"God Is Dead" and I Don't Feel So Good Myself

"God Is Dead" and I Don't Feel So Good Myself

Theological Engagements with the New Atheism

Edited by
ANDREW DAVID
CHRISTOPHER J. KELLER
& JON STANLEY

CASCADE *Books* · Eugene, Oregon

"GOD IS DEAD" AND I DON'T FEEL SO GOOD MYSELF
Theological Engagements with the New Atheism

Copyright © 2010 Wipf and Stock. All rights reserved. Except for
brief quotations in critical publications or reviews, no part of this book
may be reproduced in any manner without prior written permission
from the publisher. Write: Permissions, Wipf and Stock Publishers, 199
W. 8th Ave., Suite 3, Eugene, OR 97401.

Cascade Books
An Imprint of Wipf and Stock Publishers
199 W. 8th Ave., Suite 3
Eugene, OR 97401

www.wipfandstock.com

Cover image by Paul Roorda, "Crown of Thorns and Capeline Bandage," blood,
crushed stone, rust, gold leaf, beeswax, and vintage book pages on paper. Used by
permission.

ISBN 13: 978-1-60608-531-8

Cataloguing-in-Publication data:

"God is dead" and I don't feel so good myself : theological engagements with the
new atheism / edited by Andrew David, Christopher J. Keller, and Jon Stanley

xxii + 186 p. ; 23 cm. Includes bibliographical references.

ISBN 13: 978-1-60608-531-8

1. Christianity and atheism. 2. Faith and reason—Christianity. I. Title. II. Series.

BT1212.G5 2010

Manufactured in the U.S.A.

Contents

Contents

Preface

At a family reunion when I (Christopher) was a young boy, my mother got to talking with my estranged cousin who had left the faith. The son of a fundamentalist Christian preacher and once the golden child of his West Virginia religious community—he even achieved a brief professional career as a "Christian recording artist"—my cousin's conservative Christian faith had spiraled downward into disillusionment. He stopped attending his church, ceased reading his Bible, abandoned his daily prayer time, and committed the cardinal evangelical sin—he allowed his marriage to collapse. Repulsed by the Christian fundamentalism of his upbringing, for all intents and purposes my cousin renounced the faith.

It is this kind of narrative that today's New Atheists relish, indeed idealize: they see a recovery from *god delusions*, an enlightening exchange of the warm, fuzzy fairy tales of faith for the cold, hard facts of science. And it is a story that the New Atheism's Christian critics would decry, interpreting it as recklessly throwing the Christian baby out with the fundamentalist bathwater. But neither reaction is sensitive to the particularity of my cousin's story, nor to the theological, political, and psychological currents at play in the lives of fellow prodigals. No stories are canned—in this case, twenty years later we find that the prodigal cousin is a practicing Anglican, something neither side of the New Atheism debate would have predicted—and the truth shows itself in color rather than the black-and-white binaries of the New Atheists and their theist critics.

The New Atheism debate's explosion onto the central cultural scene presents us with a surprisingly fortuitous moment for polychromatic Christian reflection. But the fact that a virtual cottage industry has sprung up around the New Atheism debate, flooding the airwaves, op-eds, blogs, and bookshelves, made us pause and ask ourselves if we really needed another book on the New Atheism. Was there any unturned stone that if turned might make a positive contribution to a debate over which so much ink (and blood!) has already been spilled?

As we sifted through the vitriolic, reductive material coming from both sides of the debate, we concluded that it was time for an *other* kind of book, a different sort of Christian engagement with New Atheism—one that entered the debate *otherwise*, conscientiously objecting to the rules of engagement established by the generals of the culture wars, who have strategically rallied their foot soldiers through *ad hominem*, straw-man arguments and familiar talking points in ever louder and more bellicose voices. Here, we have worked hard to ignore the generals and to give you exactly this kind of book.

First, many Christian responses to popular atheism have been pedestrian, patronizing, dismissive, and violent, mirroring the New Atheists' hostility toward the Christian faith and religious culture at large. Conversely, we have sought to embody simultaneously a generous spirit, a substantive analysis, and a more incisive critique of the New Atheists (and, at times, their critics) than the market has typically produced.

Second, because most Christian responses to the New Atheism hail from conservative evangelical camps, we have assembled a bouquet of leading Christian philosophers, theologians, and writers from various confessional backgrounds. So although this book pulls no punches and makes no apology for the fact that it is a robustly *Christian* engagement with the New Atheism, the contributors vary widely in their accounts of the resurgence of this pop atheism and their assessments of what might be of value to Christians in the New Atheists' criticisms of Christian faith and religious culture.

Third, we take both the New Atheists and the debate between the New Atheists and their critics as our subject matter. The essays draw the New Atheism into dialogue with other atheisms, past and present, suggesting that some of these other atheisms might have one up on the New Atheism in terms of their social and intellectual benefit. And the essays also point out the ways in which both the New Atheists and their more conservative Christian critics often make strange bedfellows and at times even partners in crime by sharing certain problematic fundamental assumptions.

Fourth, we have chosen to engage the New Atheism not only in analytical prose, but also in creative writing and visual imagery. Indeed, poems serve as bookends to the project, intended to jumpstart the conversation and provide an alternative means of reflection. If the New

Atheism debate needs anything, it is an opening up rather than a closing down, and this collection of essays, interviews, memoir, poetry, and art is responsive to this in both form and content.

Any project we take up at *The Other Journal*—whether it's through our online quarterly, our annual film festival, or our book publications—is a product of double-vision, looking at the key issues of our day in light of the vast resources of the Christian tradition and looking at our Christian tradition in light of the key issues of our day. We believe, then, that the rise of the New Atheism provides Christians with an excellent opportunity to reflect upon and discern what is baby and what is bathwater in contemporary Christian thought, witness, and practice. It is an occasion to listen to the critiques of faith and then, as in the case of Chris's cousin, to reassess and recommit to what is at the heart of our faith, to check our idolatries at the door and scour our faith commitments with the relentless skepticism that today's popular atheists possess. This book goes out with the prayer that it might draw, compel, and even seduce believers unto a more mature faith, authentic spirituality, charitable witness, and peaceable practice.

Andrew David
Christopher J. Keller
Jon Stanley

Acknowledgments

The Other Journal is proud to partner with such creative and compelling people. Our online quarterly (http://www.theotherjournal.com), annual film festival (Film, Faith, and Justice), and book publications are all made possible by funding from Mars Hill Graduate School (MHGS) in Seattle, Washington. MHGS trains people in the study of text, soul, and culture and teaches its students to openly imagine a holistic gospel that has power to transform and save.

We would like to thank D. Stephen Long for writing a foreword that wonderfully frames the discussion we are hosting in this offering and that makes a substantive contribution to the discussion in its own right. We would also like to thank Paul Roorda for enthusiastically volunteering images from his stellar art exhibition, *The Skeptic's Gospel and Other Remedies for Truth*.

We are extremely grateful for the hard work of all our brilliant contributors and for their unique and incisive contributions to this project. You have each done us and all the other readers of this book a great service.

Finally, we would like to thank the good people at Cascade Books of Wipf & Stock Publishers for their interest in *The Other Journal* and this project. We respect your unique eye for material, your preference for meaningful content over the whims of the market, and your commitment to publishing books that combine academic rigor with broad appeal and readability.

Andrew David
Christopher J. Keller
Jon Stanley

Foreword:
Atheism's Resurgence and Christian Responses

D. Stephen Long

After the journal *Mladina* published caricatures of Muhammad, stirring irrational violent protests from some Muslims,[1] Slavoj Žižek published an editorial in the *International Herald Tribune* entitled "Atheism Is a Legacy Worth Fighting For."[2] His editorial questioned the wisdom of Dostoyevsky's putative statement, "If God is dead, everything is permitted." Far from the atheists being the source of moral atrocities, Žižek rightly noted, historically those who profess faith in God had been the ones who violated the bare minimum expectations of human decency—God gave permission for abandoning any modicum of morality altogether. The Western legacy of atheism, he then suggested, would provide a better foundation for basic goodness than had "God." For this reason Žižek "fights for" atheism.

Readers of Žižek could be excused for being confused. Five years earlier, he published a book whose subtitle asked, "Why Is the Christian Legacy Worth Fighting For?"[3] wherein he gave positive answers to this question. This seeming contradiction might confirm Charles Mathewes's counsel later in this anthology that one should only read Žižek after consuming high doses of caffeine. Nonetheless, as Mathewes notes, Žižek is an atheist Christians should read carefully, for he often speaks the truth when few others will. For instance, in his editorial he refuses "to reduce the problem of the Muhammad caricatures to one of respect for other's beliefs." He recognizes that this only patronizes people of faith, refusing

1. On February 6, 2006, *Mladina* reprinted a number of cartoons portraying Muhammad, which were originally printed on September 30, 2005, in the Danish daily newspaper *Jyllands-Posten*. Online: http://mladina.si/tednik/200606/clanek/nar --svoboda_govora-mateja_hrastar/.

2. Žižek, "Defenders of the Faith."

3. Žižek, *Fragile Absolute*.

to treat them as rational persons who are seeking truth. Thus, he also refuses to "adopt the relativist stance of multiple 'regimes of truth' disqualifying as violent imposition any clear insistence on truth." Instead, he treats religion rationally, submitting it to a common pursuit of truth, and he concludes with this suggestion, "What, however, about submitting Islam—together with all other religions—to a respectful, but for that reason no less ruthless, critical analysis?" This is atheism worth engaging.

Is all such atheism worthy of engagement? And how should Christians in particular respond to its resurgence?

No one should be surprised by its resurgence. A-theism is a parasitical consequence of the "return of religion," a return which continues to surprise persons who seem confused as to how to respond to it. The reality of faith perplexes people at the political level as well as in everyday life, as illustrated in Becky Crook's delightful story, "Mystery and Mayhem: Reading Bulgakov's *The Master and Margarita* while Dating an Atheist in Seattle." That reasonable people still have faith—and actually practice it—strikes some as odd. Many of these skeptics were convinced by the narratives spun by the great masters of suspicion, narratives insisting that the gains of the Enlightenment would surely be irreversible by the twenty-first century and that these gains would result in reasonable people eschewing belief. So how do we account for the "return" of religion (outside of universities and mainline seminaries, it never really disappeared in the first place)? Is this a pathology to be remedied, as some of the more popular atheists diagnose, whose remedies take on increasing bellicosity in inverse proportion to the strength of their arguments? Or are religious people to be considered rational and therefore engaged in the form of argument Žižek proffers? A "true atheist," he states, "has no need to boost his own stance by provoking believers with blasphemy." Truth demands something more than patronizing respect for religion or the intellectually lobotomized affirmation of religious pluralism and relativism. We Christians certainly have something to learn from atheists, but some more than others; after all, not all atheists are created equal. What follows are diverse responses to atheism's resurgence, responses that will assist readers to discern what is to be learned and what is to be avoided.

Let me suggest some *types* within which the various responses may or may not fit. This is not intended to prejudice the reader before she picks up the book, but to provoke an argument among the diverse contributors and those who might find their responses convincing.

1. Modern Atheism Is Unworthy of a Response

One response would be to dismiss modern atheism (or certain versions of it) altogether. Take for instance Peter Candler's opening analysis of the atheism of Richard Dawkins, Christopher Hitchens, Sam Harris, and Michael Onfray. Candler writes, "Suffice it to say that if this gang of atheists represents the highest form of atheism these days, and if every atheism is always parasitic upon some form of theism, then the critiques of religion offered in these books imply that the state of theology in public discourse is pretty dismal" (83–84). Candler offers less a response to the so-called New Atheism and more a critique of contemporary theology. He does not explain why Dawkins so badly understands the ontological argument or misunderstands Wittgenstein; such a response would be too easy. A more worthy response, he suggests, is to question ourselves; the weaknesses of the arguments for the resurgent atheism are less to be taken seriously than to provoke theological self-criticism. Why have our accounts of who God is not produced a more interesting reaction? If we are to have an atheist the caliber of Nietzsche rather than Dawkins, we will have to do better with our reasons for faith. Of course, that these resurgent atheists have sought to avoid parasitism by changing their names from "a-theists" to "brighties" only demonstrates that the same kitsch we find in so much contemporary Christian worship and music now has its correlate in the New Atheism.

2. Variations on Dostoyevsky

Žižek challenges Dostoyevsky's assertion that God's death brings down the walls of restraint against immorality. But another version of Dostoyevsky's assertion might go like this: "If God is dead, everything is atomized." It is not so much that everything is permitted, but that everything is flattened, everything is placed on the same immanent plane and reduced to its barest elements. In a witty albeit sobering play on the "atomization" in modern politics and science, Andy Barnes observes the reality of slums in the Philippines and suggests that "if there is no God, no second life, and no redemption, then there is no hope for these slums, because too much has been lost already. Everything is rising entropy, decomposition, and atomization, and there's no way to glorify that here" (101). He challenges atheist materialists by asking, can you look upon the atomized reality of decomposition and say, "Yes"? Implicit in his challenge is another theme that runs through many of these essays: materialism without God becomes nothing but atomized decomposition. Or to put it less delicately, is the true end of man nothing but shit? Have we lost our sense of smell?

3. Atheism as Apophaticism

To a certain extent, Robert Inchausti and Merold Westphal welcome the resurgent atheism, for the 'god' denied in this atheism is not the God we Christians affirm. Drawing upon Thomas Merton's apology to unbelievers, Inchausti finds believers responsible for the unbelief of our neighbors. By setting forth an unflattering presentation of God and exhibiting actions that run contrary to the very God they affirm, believers are the ones responsible for the construction of a 'god' whose deconstruction by atheists actually does theology a service.

Westphal takes a similar line, wisely reminding us that something more than proofs or disproofs for the existence of God are at the heart of the matter for contemporary atheists. Few of us, he suggests, came to faith through such proofs. After all, who knew the ontological proof for the existence of God or Aquinas's "five ways" before he or she was already a convinced Christian? And how many atheists were not already well on their way to losing faith before reading Hitchens or Dawkins? We were already long down the road toward faith or disbelief before these arguments could sway us one way or another. Westphal rejects that what is at stake in the current debates are convincing arguments for theism. If we can admit that few of us came to faith because of such commanding reasons, then might it not also be the case that what drives atheists is also something other than rational arguments alone? If Westphal is correct, then the appropriate response to atheism is not better arguments, but a patient humility borne from penitential disciplines. He urges Christians, with some important qualifications, to adopt a "hermeneutic of suspicion" as a Lenten discipline.

Westphal finds an ally here in Charles Taylor who, like Candler, finds much of modern atheism "intellectually shoddy." Taylor argues that one reason for this is the assumption "that there really are some knockdown arguments against belief in God" (126). He then places this peculiar version of modern atheism in its historical context, in the rise of a scientism that claims it can explain everything: "And of course, this is something you can only believe if you have a scientistic, reductionist conception and explanation of everything in the world, including human beings. If you do have such a view that everything is to be explained in terms of physics and the movement of atoms and the like, then certain forms of access to God are just closed" (126). (Incidentally, I recommend reading Taylor while watching John Cleese's "The Scientist at Work" podcast on the "discovery" of the God gene. Cleese says, "The discovery of this God gene is a big step forward in our quest to show that every bit of human behavior can be explained mechanically because we have now also located the gene that makes some people believe that every piece of human behavior can be explained mechanically, and it is here right next to the gene that makes you go to Nicholas Cage movies."[4]) Thus, a proper response to resurgent atheism will not be found in stronger theistic arguments, but in a broader conception of rationality itself, one that will recognize that the rigid boundaries erected between faith and reason are much more porous than scientism, as well as much of modern epistemology, could recognize. Such scientism did not discover some rigid boundary between faith and reason; it erected it. Ronald A. Kuipers seeks to explain such a position to an acquaintance as a way to advance the conversation: "For example, I could take the time to explain to her that, not only am I religious, but I have been trained in an intellectual tradition that rejects the Enlightenment belief in the possibility of religious neutrality, that is, of anyone not being religious in some sense" (146).

Jon Stanley offers another version of this position, although he is less concerned with the arguments for and against God's existence, and more interested in analyzing faith as always containing an element of doubt. He reminds us that whenever we confess our belief, we at the same time pray for assistance with our unbelief: "I do believe, help me overcome my unbelief!" (Mark 9:24 NIV). This is authentic faith, for it acknowledges the element of a-theism present in our confession. Stanley helps us understand why we often suspect that those who confess most loudly are simultaneously trying to silence that other voice, which whispers, "I do not exist." For Stanley, that voice may not come only from the devil, not least because the philosophical category of "existence" may be an improper predicate for the God of Abraham, Isaac, and Jacob. In fact, the

4. Cleese, "Scientist at Work."

god in which we doubt may be a specific example of faith because most of the gods we construct are idols—take for instance Thor, the god who we often affirm in our recitations of the United States' pledge of allegiance, or Dionysius, the god of liberal affirmation. To learn to doubt these gods' existence is itself a species of faith. Stanley wants Christians to be mistaken for atheists much as the early Christians were when they denied the gods of the Roman Empire. Stanley will find an ally here in Westphal, who confesses that he "had probably never prayed to a God who wasn't an idol" (77). Westphal's affirmation of Luther and Stanley's affirmation of Derrida bear a striking resemblance. Both assume that much of Christian tradition produced a metaphysical idol that needs deconstruction.

4. Outnarration of Modern Atheism

John Milbank also emphasizes the importance of the *apophatic* tradition and the inevitable relation between faith and reason. Yet his response to atheism takes a slightly different angle than that of Inchausti, Westphal, Taylor, Kuipers, and Stanley. Milbank's intent is less to dismiss or welcome modern atheism and more to recognize its cultural and/or metaphysical presuppositions and then outnarrate them. He does not provide much of that narrative here, but he points to his and others' work that has tried to do so. Resurgent atheism has a cultural history, and as he puts it, "To my mind, then, modernity is liberalism, liberalism is capitalism—'political economy'—and capitalism is atheism and nihilism" (63). Connections should be demonstrated among a-theism and the political and material conditions of late modernity, but Milbank currently finds little ability among the Left to offer the critical analysis that is necessary. Instead, theology has to play this role: "The hard thing now for critical thinkers to do is to think outside leftism. They have to see that if neoliberalism and neoconservatism have totally triumphed, this is because the Left in its traditional mode is incapable of carrying out an adequate critique of capitalism. In the end, this is because it's atheistic—one needs to be religious to recognize objective values and meanings as not just epiphenomenal" (65).

Stanley and Suriano disagree on the usefulness of Derridean atheism for Christianity. This reveals a significant, albeit subtle, difference between them in regard to how they believe Christians should think about metaphysics, as well as the traditional understanding of God. Suriano, like Milbank, shows how materialist atheism cannot adequately account for the very materialism it rightly affirms. He attempts to outnarrate atheism as opposed to welcoming it as a deconstruction of the idols of our own making. But these two positions should not be decisively set against each other; they bear a formal resemblance. Stanley uses Derridean deconstruction to challenge the idols Christians construct; Suriano then raises ontological questions about this use of Derrida, challenging the Christian use of deconstruction and warning that deconstructionist thought might sneak those same idols back in through the very method applied. They have a similar end, but they differ in their analysis of how to achieve it. Suriano denies that this kind of atheism can in any sense be liberatory or a challenge to idols, insisting instead that it "perpetuates an ideological, and therein idolatrous, construction—one that is itself not a progressive coming-of-age or a sobering up, but rather the preservation and refinement of a pagan trajectory of power seeking" (28). When we become certain that we cannot know God, that the finite a priori has no capacity to receive the divine, then every positive naming of God's appearance must always be accompanied by a corresponding dis-appearance (here once again, Luther's *sub contrario* and Derrida's *difference* may find common cause). Although this might appear a properly modest and humble theological assertion, it brings with it an ontology that hides menacing arrogance: that ontology is the dominance of the will and its power to construct and deconstruct. It is the *nihil*, which is the god behind God, to which even God must bow. Because of this, Suriano does not find it appropriate to welcome even the more sophisticated forms of atheism that one finds in Derrida. He states, "Consequently, what we find is that a world of mere power without God (a-theos) is not one where desire is jovially liberated into heightened possibilities, nor is it a celebration of life where everything is permitted, as it is often advertised. Rather, it is a world set loose only to simultaneously enclose itself within an iron cage of cold instrumental rationality" (36).

Like Žižek, Suriano does not find Dostoyevsky compelling. Far from everything being permitted, when God is dead, less and less is permitted, for everything must now be accountable to a cost-benefit calculation that arises from the dominance of the ontology he finds at the base of modern atheism. Here we can learn from yet another important atheist, Nietzsche, who helped in part to make such a diagnosis. Nietzsche quipped, "Those who lose God, cling all the more tightly to morality."[5] Could it be that modern atheism narrows the pursuit of the good to such an extent that it reduces the forms of life permissible to only those that can adopt its rigid moral calculation and pass its standard? Dawkins is certainly right. You do not need God for morality. But the morality he and Peter Singer advocate may not need a great deal else as well.

Another version of outnarration, which nicely parallels Westphal's claim that little of the current debate has to do with rational arguments qua reason alone, is Randal Rauser's essay on worshipping teapots. Like Candler, Rauser does not find the rational arguments of the New Atheists worthy of response—at least not in terms of reason alone. As he puts it, "To be frank, the sophistication of their respective critiques is closer to the level of the crude village atheist or the curmudgeonly troll who emerges from under his bridge to throw stones at passing parishioners. The New Atheism is notable not for the power of its argumentation, but rather for the heightened intensity of its rhetoric" (131). But of course village atheists, like psychics, creationists, day traders, and therapists armed with Myers-Briggs tests, can do no end of harm. For this reason, Rauser advocates a move away from a response akin to the analytic philosophy of reason, where we might win the "logical" argument but lose altogether "plausibility," and a move toward a "background framework" that abandons the Christian kitsch of bumper stickers, action figure dolls, and Thomas Kinkade paintings. Such a move requires taking the role of art, music, literature, and architecture seriously, thereby rendering our Christian witness as intellectually sound.

The above four types are finally not distinct and exclusive such that one should choose among them. The thinkers I have listed under these types could easily be shuffled about and identified in more than one type. Moreover, the rich essays, interviews, and poetry that make up this collection provide a much greater variety of responses than those I note here. I only hope to begin the conversation and to assert that much as the problem with modern atheism is, as Taylor notes, its desire to reduce everything to a single, causal explanation, so our response has to be much richer. Life cannot be reduced to a principle of economy. *The Other Journal* has done a marvelous service in offering us this rich analysis. They will

5. Nietzsche, *Will to Power*, 16; my translation.

most likely change very few minds, but they might guide those who seek that which is true and good. Moreover, those who are still seeking such an end might find that theology can affirm their pursuit. Or perhaps this introduction should end with the boldness Milbank calls for—indeed, it is "only theology" that can render such a journey intelligible.

1

Praise Him

Brad Davis

As for idols, they are impotent. Not
one can see or speak or feel

a neighbor's ache—her dog dead
and child missing below the levee. I read

headlines and feel more
than all the idols that there ever were.

Even the idol that is our idea
of God is impotent—B is not A—

yet God does what he pleases,
the earth what is true to its nature.

We build cities and pay scant attention
to either, then cry foul when the dam breaks.

Idols cannot save, nor theologies.
Only God, and that is no great comfort.

2

Thomas Merton's Apologies to an Unbeliever

ROBERT INCHAUSTI

*Believing means liberating the indestructible element in oneself, or,
more accurately, being indestructible, or, more accurately, being.*
   —Kafka's Diaries

Two years before his death, the Trappist monk and best-selling author
Thomas Merton published an essay addressed to unbelievers that apolo-
gized for the inadequacy and impertinence of what had been inflicted
upon them in the name of religion. He felt compelled to write not just
because the manipulative antics and "vaudeville" of the defenders of the
faith embarrassed him but also because it seemed to him that their "defenses" constituted "a falsification of religious truth"[1]:

> Faith comes by hearing, says Saint Paul, but by hearing what? The
> cries of snake-handlers? The soothing platitudes of the religious
> operator? One must be able to listen to the inscrutable ground of
> (one's) own being, and who am I to say that (the atheists') reserva-
> tions about religious commitment do not protect, in [them], this
> kind of listening? ... While I certainly believe that the message of
> the Gospel is something that we are called upon to preach, I think
> we will communicate it more intelligently in dialogue.[2]

Merton approached this dialogue by asserting that there is no choice between faith and science, that there is no choice between Christ and the

---

1. Merton, "Apologies to an Unbeliever"; first published in *Harper's Magazine*, 36–39;
cited here in Merton, *Faith and Violence*, 205–6.

2. Ibid., 210.

world. According to Merton, we can only choose Christ by choosing the world as it really is in him and encountered by us in the ground of our own personal freedom and love. God is not an object, thing, or external reality, but Being itself—the ground of all that exists, which includes atheists and theists. Thus, atheists exist in God, just as Christians do; it's just that they do not refer to the ground of their being as "God," if they refer to it at all.

In his essay "The Contemplative and the Atheist," Merton honors the honest confusion of atheists struggling against their own infantile conception of God:

> Many who consider themselves atheists are in fact persons who are discontented with the naïve idea of God which makes him appear to be an "object" or a "thing" in a merely finite and human sense. . . . [But] those who are familiar with the apophatic tradition in theology and mysticism are fully aware that the temporary or permanent inability to imagine God or to "experience" him as present, or even to find him credible, is not something discovered by modern man or confined to our own age.[3]

Indeed, the life of the Christian contemplative is not a life of willful concentration upon a few clear and comforting ideas but a life of inner struggle in which the monk, like Christ in the desert, is tested. Perhaps we might learn from Merton and the apophatic tradition—first found in the works of Gregory of Nyssa—that to talk about God using any positive attributions of what God "is like" is too limited to do justice to the fullness of the divine mystery. The apophatic tradition, sometimes referred to as "negative theology," affirms God by questioning any and all human categories and positive theological systems. Such an approach might serve as a bridge between atheists and Christians. In fact, even the atheistic evangelist Sam Harris acknowledges the possibility of an agnostic spirituality, a secular phenomenology that takes religious experience seriously, even if it finds the idea of a God problematic.[4]

Although Merton had an in-depth correspondence with Eric Fromm, an atheist whose work reflects an openness to religious dialogue, Merton died before he could begin a serious conversation between believers and unbelievers. In the years following his death—the late seventies and

---

3. Merton, *Contemplation in a World of Action*, 168.
4. See the last half of Harris, *End of Faith*.

eighties—religious people launched an offensive against secular society, science, and atheism. Their primary weapon was reductive biblical literalism (or biblicism), and this passionate doctrinal rigidity ultimately gave birth to the backlash of militant atheisms we are now currently experiencing.

In recent years Christopher Hitchens, Richard Dawkins, Sam Harris, and others have published bestselling polemics against Christianity using little or no recognition of the apophatic tradition or the contemplative dimension of Scripture. The combative tenor of these books is no doubt a response to the onslaught of twenty-plus years of know-nothing pop apologetics that has so polarized and dumbed down the national conversation concerning faith that when I read these books, I find myself agreeing with almost everything they say.

And yet at the same time, I also find in them the flawed logic of the straw man fallacy. The god they do not believe in is certainly not a god I ever believed in, and the "believers" they attack strike me as insecure, faithless souls who use religion as a drug to sooth their anxieties or a club to beat those with whom they disagree. Confident persons of faith do not reject scientific discoveries, secular wisdom, or open dialogue. In fact, such things can be seen as the very fruits of faith, not its antitheses. Merton believed that the religious problem of the twentieth century was twofold: (1) atheists identify faith itself with the most mindless expressions of religious fanatics, and (2) the "faith" many "believers" have kept is sentimental and self-aggrandizing—substituting comfortable, cultural illusions and cheap grace for the challenges. The first 1,500 years of the church reveal a deeper and more sustainable contemplative faith than what too often passes for contemporary apologetics.[5]

"What [the Christian contemplative] learns," Merton explains, "is not a clearer idea of God but a deeper trust, a purer love, and a more complete abandonment to One he knows to be beyond all understanding."[6] Yet in this abandonment, the contemplative has access to values that the contemporary atheist tends to forget, underestimate, or ignore. These values include a healthy skepticism toward abstract reductionism and scientism, sympathy for the paradoxical nature of truth and its existential and experiential expression, and appreciation for the literary and figurative nature of the mind.

5. See Merton, "Apologies to an Unbeliever."
6. Merton, *Contemplation*, 163.

The apophatic experience of God as *unknowable* does to some extent verify the atheist's view that God is not an object of precise knowledge and so consequently cannot be apprehended as a thing to be studied. But where the atheist's experience of God is purely negative, the experience of the apophatic contemplative is, as Merton puts it, "negatively *positive*."[7] That is to say, the believer responds to our cognitive limitations with an inward turn, whereas the nonbeliever redoubles his calculative ambitions. It is almost as if the believer is more skeptical than the skeptic in that he is skeptical of concepts themselves. Thus, in relinquishing any attempt to grasp God in limited human terms, faith reveals itself as the ground of human experience in the ground of being. "Here," Merton notes, "we enter a realm of apparent contradiction which eludes clear explanation, so that contemplatives prefer not to talk about it at all. Indeed in the past, serious mistakes have been made and deadly confusion has arisen from inadequate attempts to explain this mystery."[8] This is why the Tao that can be named is not the eternal Tao and why Saint John of the Cross finds the fullest expression of his experience of the divine in *nothing*.[9]

It may seem that the mystics are making the skeptics' point, when in fact they are announcing an ontological turn. To the question, "How do you know God exists?" They reply, "Who is asking?" This is not an evasion but a shift in perspective—as we can see in any good poet, psychoanalyst, or Zen master, the first step in the deepening of awareness is to question the illusory ground upon which the autonomous, modern self holds forth. And the mystics hope to swap epistemological priorities for psychological and ontological ones. If the skeptic fails to take this move seriously or, alternatively, if the believer refuses to acknowledge the validity (albeit narrow in range) of the skeptic's reductionist outlook, then the dialogue is over and polemics ensue.

When Merton wrote his "Apology to an Unbeliever" in 1968, he thought that it was time for the Christian consciousness of God to be expressed in more contemporary language. He felt that the medieval ideas of God, which were based on medieval ideas about the cosmos, earth, physics, and the biological and psychological structure of man, were clearly

7. Ibid., 172; italics added.

8. Ibid., 168–69.

9. For a deft introduction to the ideas of Saint John of the Cross, see Kavanaugh, introduction.

out of date, but that "the reality of experience beyond concepts, however, is not itself modified by changes of culture."[10] This focus upon experience reflects the views of our best cognitive scientists and brain researchers, who have revealed the psychopathology of everyday life to be a biological given. A focus on experience also gives the contemplative an advantage over the theologian in mapping the wisdom of the New Testament against the conceptual structures of contemporary art and science.

By focusing upon the reality of *experiences*, conventional logic and dualistic thinking are overcome, and Christ becomes a living, inclusive, existential Messiah—not a cipher in a questionable cosmological construct. Faith ceases to be a mad embrace of superstitions and is revealed as the healthy recognition of a mystery within which both our language and our intellects must humbly submit. "If the deepest ground of our being is love," Merton writes, "then in that very love itself and nowhere else will I find myself, and the world, and my brother, and Christ. It is not a question of either/or but all-in-one."[11]

The contemplative Christian reads Scripture as icon, image, and poetry—not just rhetoric, argument, and assertion. Skepticism is not the only intellectual virtue—but rather only one part of a whole range of intellectual activities including theory, application, speculation, and imagination. The dumbing down of Scripture to its supposed literal dogmatic core is a creature of the modern predilection to reduction, which can lead to some absurd readings of Scripture for both believers and skeptics.

Nonbelievers have a little harder time extricating themselves from this impasse because so many of them operate on the assumption that Being itself is a false category, and so there is nothing meaningful for the text itself to point to other than empirical facts. The images fall flat, the narratives are reduced to moral fables, and the larger critique of cultural mythology disappears—replaced by a series of tired, culturally derived empirical attributes. For the contemplative, however, biblical narratives and images speak of a different relationship to the cosmos than the merely factual and to a different relationship to one's own mind, emotions, identity, community, and current cultural mythology.

So, in the end, Merton would agree with those atheists who deny God's existence as some sort of super "decider," concept, or thing, but

10. Merton, *Contemplation*, 172.

11. Ibid., 155–56.

he would disagree with those who then draw the conclusion that God, therefore, does not exist. What does not exist is the God-object. What does exist is a presence revealed in and through the love that rises in us out of a ground that lies beyond us.

Merton explains that his calling as a monk and Christian contemplative changes the role doubt plays in his life:

> My own peculiar task in my Church and in my world has been that of the solitary explorer who, instead of jumping on all the latest bandwagons at once, is bound to search the existential deaths of faith in its silences, its ambiguities, and in those certainties which lie deeper than the bottom of anxiety. In these depths there are no easy answers, no pat solutions to anything. It is a kind of submarine life in which faith sometimes mysteriously takes on the aspect of doubt when, in fact, one has to doubt and reject conventional surrogates that have taken the place of faith. On this level, the division between Believer and Unbeliever ceases to be so crystal clear.[12]

The self-questioning, if honestly and sincerely embraced, exposes religious sentimentality and prepares the way for a deeper, disillusioned knowledge of God:

> The most hopeful sign of religious renewal is the authentic sincerity and openness with which some Believers are beginning to recognize this [need for the faithful to doubt cheap grace and pop theology]. At the very moment when it would seem that they had to gather for a fanatical last-ditch stand, these Believers are dropping their defensiveness, their defiance, and their mistrust. They are realizing that a faith that is afraid of other people is not faith at all. A faith that supports itself by condemning others is itself condemned by the Gospel.[13]

One thinks of the proverbial atomic scientist who knew a new idea in physics was important by the fact that it terrified him. The same could be said for a new experience of the divine in prayer, for faith, like science, is not always comforting. As the Gospels make clear, it is demanding, challenging, and open to paradigm-shattering revelations.

As the poet Rilke says, "We fling our emptiness out of our arms into the spaces we breathe so that the birds might feel the expanded air with

---

12. Merton, "Apologies to an Unbeliever," 213.

13. Ibid., 213–14.

more passionate flying."[14] This courageous self-giving—open to believer and unbeliever alike—represents the new culture that is emerging on the far side of the modernist divide between atheism and superstition. This is the culture where every practicing contemplative, mystic, and true scientist has always labored, and now that the skeptics have vented some of their resentments and the reactionary Christians have had their say, perhaps a real conversation about our place in the cosmos can begin—free from invective, straw-man arguments, and polemical grandstanding.

14. This is a paraphrase from Rilke's "First Elegy," 5.

3

Why Every Christian Should "Quite Rightly Pass for an Atheist"

Jon Stanley

Only an atheist can be a good Christian.
  —Ernst Bloch

Only a Christian can be a good atheist.
  —Jürgen Moltmann

I quite rightly pass for an atheist.
  —Jacques Derrida

On Passing for an Atheist along with Derrida

When the late French post-structuralist philosopher Jacques Derrida confessed, "I quite rightly pass for an atheist,"[1] it raised quite a stir—to say the least. This was not the first of Derrida's devilishly pithy comments,

---

1. Derrida, "Circumfession," 154–55. The immediate context of the statement is worth quoting: "[T]hat's what my readers won't have known about me . . . my writing . . . to be bound better and better but be read less and less well over almost twenty years, like my religion about which nobody understands anything, any more than does my mother who asked other people a while ago, not daring to talk to me about it, if I still believed in God . . . but she must have known that the constancy of God in my life is called by other names, so that I quite rightly pass for an atheist, the omnipresence to me of what I call God in my absolved, absolutely private language being neither that of an eyewitness nor that of a voice doing anything other than talking to me without saying anything, nor a transcendent law or immanent *schechina*, that feminine figure of Yahweh who remains so strange and so familiar to me, but the secret I am excluded from."

but it remains one of his most provocative. Some have interpreted his confession as a veiled reference to being either an atheist or a theist, a final coming clean, coming out, or getting off the fence. And those who take it so matter-of-factly either celebrate that Derrida came out on "our side" or lament that he went to the "dark side." Of course, one's response depends on which side of the fence one happens to be standing, and which side one interprets Derrida as leaning toward. It should be no surprise, then, that celebration and lamentation, name-calling and praise, are found in both atheistic and theistic camps. After all, Derrida has been branded "heretic" and "saint" by atheist and theist alike.

We humans have a penchant for categorization and classification. In itself, there is nothing wrong with this. In fact, it can be a quite pleasurable and beneficial activity. Witness children classifying images of barnyard animals according to their kind. Not only does this bring them a certain amount of pleasure—children often giggle as they classify—but it also furthers their ability to navigate the world, providing them with the conceptual skills they need to find their way through all the zoos of life. Thank God for child's play!

When it comes to classifying, it seems that out of all the things in God's good creation, nothing provides us more *jouissance* than classifying other people—as this, that, or the other. In itself, there is nothing wrong with this either. Consider the pleasure that comes from recognizing and honoring cultural differences, and the benefit of discerning those to whom we shall entrust ourselves in friendship. However, there is also a shadow side to classifying people. The pleasure of classification can become quite devilish when we are overcome by the desire to rigidly group people along hard lines and lump them into categories that do not quite suit them.[2]

In postmodern lingo, such sweeping and blunt categorizations represent a failure to honor the "singularity" (or one-of-a-kindness) of individuals, a reduction of their "alterity" (or otherness) to familiar categories, and an obfuscation of the "irreducible mystery" that each person

---

2. Classification becomes particularly devilish in the case of demonization, which occurs when someone is categorized as evil and therefore identified with evil per se. For example, despite the ideological gap between ex-president George W. Bush and Saddam Hussein, Bush's naming of Hussein as an "evil dictator" and Hussein's naming of Bush as the "great Satan" were likely instances of demonization rather than helpful categorization.

ultimately is, even to her/himself. However, the notion that every person (indeed, every thing) is <u>irreducibly mysterious</u> has a place in the history of thought long before the postmoderns came on the scene. In his *Confessions*, Saint Augustine writes, "But I beg you, O Lord my God, to look upon me and listen to me. Have pity on me and heal me, for you see that *I have become a problem* [*or mystery*] *to myself.*"[3] The ethical implication of this ontological and epistemological insight is that if we are ultimately even "mysteries to ourselves," then we should be all the more careful in our classification of others and in our claims to know who they really are and what they are all about.[4]

I am reminded of the time my grandfather came to live with my parents after he was diagnosed with Alzheimer's disease. During that time, my mother would check in daily with my grandfather to see how his illness was progressing. One morning during breakfast, she asked him quite directly, "Grandpa Dewey, do you know who I am?" His response was of the sort that our family has since come to describe as "classic Grandpa Dewey." In his thick Southern drawl, he incredulously replied, "Lady, if you don't know who you are, then how in the hell am I supposed to know?" My grandfather, with his grade school education, had in one line summed up Augustine's sentiment more succinctly than any postmodern theoretician I have ever read.

This burning desire to penetrate the mystery of the *other*, to know who they really are, could be characterized as a case of classification fever,[5] and our age seems to be suffering from it in epidemic proportions. Interestingly, it seems that this fever rages more strongly in some areas of life than others. For example, we are all familiar with the adage, "Never talk about religion and politics over dinner." I would argue that this has become the conventional wisdom of the day because religion and politics are two areas where classification fever burns the hottest.

3. Augustine *Confessions* X.33 (p. 239); italics added.

4. For a sampling of how Augustine's notion that we are "questions to ourselves" has been taken up in contemporary postmodern philosophical hermeneutics and ethics, respectively, see Caputo, *More Radical Hermeneutics*, and Kristeva, *Strangers to Ourselves*.

5. I am playing on Derrida's notion of "archive fever," which is used in his critique of Freudian psychoanalysis. Derrida refers to archive fever as "a compulsive, repetitive, and nostalgic desire for the archive, an irrepressible desire to return to the origin, a homesickness, a nostalgia for the return to the most archaic place of absolute commencement" (Derrida, *Archive Fever*, 19).

Perhaps we will tolerate some level of ambiguity when it comes to politics. After all, it may be perfectly legitimate to be torn between being either a Republican or a Democrat. But this degree of ambivalence is rarely tolerated when it comes to religion. Being torn between being either an atheist or a theist, or confessing one's discomfort with the categories themselves, is usually interpreted as weak-willed, weak-minded, or both. When it comes to religion, we want tall sturdy fences, and we do not want anyone riding them, so you better get off, thank you very much! There is something in us that demands to know at the end of the day, and after a thousand qualifications, whether someone is either a "theist" or an "atheist." And as the arguments between atheists and theists to prove the existence or non-existence of God fly back and forth on talk radio, in the op-eds, and in the *New York Times* Best Seller list, the fever is spreading.

Yet it is precisely this raging curiosity that Derrida would not satisfy with a straightforward answer. For those philosophers and theologians suffering from classification fever, it would have been so comforting if Derrida had simply said, "I am a theist," or "I am an atheist," but instead, he offered this subtle and suggestive credo: "I quite rightly pass for an atheist."[6] Perhaps he was attempting to "break" the fever.

Derrida himself speaks of "my religion about which nobody understands anything,"[7] and I will take him at his word. Notice the similar sentiment in the words of Augustine, who, even after over three hundred pages of spiritual autobiography, confesses:

> But many people who know me, and others who do not know me but have heard of me or read my books, wish to hear what I am now, at this moment, and yet it is in my heart that I am whatever I am. So they wish to listen as I confess what I am in my heart, into which they cannot pry by eye or ear or mind. They wish to hear and they are ready to believe; *but can they really know me?*[8]

Once again, if both Augustine and Derrida ultimately remain a question to themselves, then in the words of my grandfather, "How in the hell are we supposed to know who they really are?"

---

6. Derrida, "Circumfession," 155.

7. Ibid., 154.

8. Augustine *Confessions* X.3 (p. 209); italics added.

Derrida has also continually drawn attention to the "porous bound-aries" between atheism and theism. Leaning on the apophatic tradition of negative theology, he speaks of a certain type of theism that "at times so resembles a profession of atheism as to be mistaken for it," as well as a certain form of atheism that has "always testified to the most intense de-sire for God."[9] One gets the sense that Derrida is uncomfortable with the categories themselves, and although he is no champion of the American individualistic spirit, at least with respect to religion, one can read be-tween the lines a certain, "Don't fence me in!" This is all the more reason it would be odd to take Derrida's comment as any kind of rubber stamp on the typical way the lines between atheism and theism have been drawn, let alone as an unqualified endorsement of one over the other. In fact, speaking of those who rustle through his writings trying to find evidence to peg him as either a theist or an atheist, Derrida notes how "strange" it is to him that "they situate me everywhere among the two."[10]

So, rather than joining the grand inquisition that demands to know whether at the end of the day Derrida was either this or that (I will leave that to those with classification fever), I will take a different tack on Derrida's comment. John Caputo, one of the premiere figures in conti-nental philosophy of religion, suggests that, rather than making a veiled atheistic or theistic claim, Derrida is drawing attention to the structure of belief/unbelief itself, as that which always underlies any particular claim, including atheistic and theistic claims. In this way, Derrida was avoiding and critiquing the dogmatism that applies equally to any strong atheistic or strong theistic claim that fails to acknowledge that whatever one be-lieves, belief and unbelief are always inextricably linked.[11] This may at first sound like an affront to believing ears, but Derrida—or at least Caputo's gloss on Derrida—is actually echoing a very biblical notion. In biblical terms, authentic faith is not characterized by the denial of one's doubt and unbelief, but by acknowledging it (even owning it); authentic faith means

---

9. See Derrida, *On the Name*, especially 35–36. The kind of atheism that testifies "to the most intense desire for God" resonates with what the German theologian Jürgen Moltmann has described as "an atheis[m] for God's sake," in which the believer "destroys all images, traditions, and religious feelings . . . that unite him with God in an illusive fashion . . . for the sake of the inexpressibly living, wholly different God" (Moltmann, "Introduction," 28).

10. Derrida, "Villanova," 99.

11. Caputo, *Philosophy and Theology*, 62.

joining the father of the boy who had just been healed by Jesus in praying, "I believe, I don't believe, help my unbelief" (Mark 9:24).[12]

For Christians to confess that they "quite rightly pass for atheists" is to admit that they do not make good "true believers," the kind of sure-footed believers that have no tolerance for doubt. But not being good true believers does not mean that they cannot believe truly. Those who believe truly are honest about their unbelief and therefore live with a confidence that is guided by the knowledge of faith rather than the expectation of rational certainty. Such a faith-knowledge is qualified by trust (or *troth*), and trust always demands a certain level of risk. "I believe, I don't believe, help my unbelief"—this is the prayer of those who believe truly, and it is in this sense that Christians can confess that at times they quite rightly pass for atheists.

But Caputo highlights another dimension of Derrida's devilish little comment. Caputo hears in Derrida echoes of the Danish (Christian) philosopher Søren Kierkegaard. Kierkegaard would never refer to himself as *being* a Christian per se, not because it would have been more accurate to refer to himself as something else (an agnostic, Muslim, or Buddhist, for example), but because he would only go so far as to say he was in the process of *becoming* a Christian. As Kierkegaard writes:

> If I must be candid, I do not deny that I am not a Christian in the New Testament sense; if I must be honest, I do not deny that my life cannot be called an effort *in the direction* of what the New Testament calls Christianity, *in the direction* of denying myself, renouncing the world, dying from it, etc.; rather the earthly and the temporal become more and more important to me with every year I live.[13]

This confession is quite personal, yet Kierkegaard is also speaking beyond himself. He suggests that this is what "every single [Christian] individual" would say if he were "honest enough with God and with himself."[14] Bracketing Kierkegaard's self-denying and world-renouncing spirituality for the moment, the point I want to highlight is that, for Kierkegaard, being

---

12. My paraphrase. The NIV translation reads, "Immediately the boy's father exclaimed, 'I do believe; help me overcome my unbelief!'"

13. Kierkegaard, *Attack upon Christendom*, 30; italics added.

14. Ibid.

a Christian means orienting one's life-effort in a particular direction,[15] "in the direction of what the New Testament calls Christianity," or becoming like Christ. Accordingly, if every Christian were honest, they would have to admit that even on their best days, they do not make very good ones.

For Kierkegaard, the virtues that characterize someone who recognizes that they are always becoming a Christian are humility and rigor: the humility of admitting that we have not fully arrived at Christ-likeness, and the rigor of a wholehearted pursuit of becoming like Christ. Kierkegaard would contrast these virtues with the vices of pride and sloth, which characterize someone who claims to have arrived at being a Christian—full stop. In this way, we might see Bonhoeffer's critique of the German Christians' cheapening of grace as echoing Kierkegaard's critique of the Christendom of his day. Both Kierkegaard and Bonhoeffer were all too aware of the danger of Christians who fail to acknowledge that they are always in process and that grace must not be pitted against the humble effort that becoming more like Christ requires.

Caputo interprets Derrida's vigilance in denying *being* this, that, or whatever, by way of Kierkegaard's vigilance in honoring the fact that he was always in the process of *becoming*. Now, this is not to say that Derrida was admitting to becoming a Christian in the straightforward sense, merely that, like Kierkegaard, he recognized the inauthenticity and danger of the "true believer" who suffers from arrested development by claiming to have arrived at a final religious conclusion, interpretation, or state of the journey. Once again, Derrida was drawing attention to the structure of religious faith and the formula for religious confession— whether we identify ourselves as theists, atheists, agnostics, Christians, Muslims, Buddhists, or Jews, we are always in the process of becoming whatever we claim to be.[16]

Once again, this is a sentiment with which Christians should be familiar. If we can confess with the Apostle Paul that in striving to become

15. One hears echoes here of Friedrich Nietzsche's notion that a worthwhile life requires an "obedience over a long period of time and in a single direction" (*Beyond Good and Evil*, 101). You might recognize this from the title, drawn from Nietzsche, of Eugene Peterson's spiritual classic *A Long Obedience in the Same Direction*.

16. The ontological principle guiding this discussion of the being/becoming relation is that *structure* (being) and *genesis* (becoming) are best understood as correlates or co-related features of creaturely existence. For this reason, the Christian philosopher James H. Olthuis speaks of human existence in terms of "be(com)ing"; see Olthius, "Be(com)-ing Humankind as Gift and Call."

like Christ we "press on toward that which we have not obtained" (Phil 3:12),[17] then I believe that in the presence of those who claim to have arrived, the Christian who believes truly will quite rightly pass for less than a true believer. And once again, that is a very good (and very biblical) thing! As Caputo writes, "Might it be that the best formula available to believers who are sensitive to the complex and multiple forces that are astir within us, as we all should be, is to claim that at most they 'rightly pass' for a believer? Is this not an excellent formula for whatever we believe or do not believe?"[18]

In our current religiously charged atmosphere, where the fever for religious classification runs strong and where the inquiry into one's religious identity is often (quite literally) a *loaded* question, we could learn something from (Caputo's gloss on) Derrida's comment. Given Derrida's account of the structure of religious faith and the formula for religious confession, whatever we (as theists, atheists, agnostics, Christians, Muslims, Buddhists, or Jews) happen to *believe*, we must admit that we are always both *believers and unbelievers*. And whatever we claim to *be*, we must admit that we are always in the process of *becoming*. Following Kierkegaard, Derrida, and Caputo, given today's environment, perhaps the most honest and wise way to answer the question "Are you a believer?" is to say, "I'd really like to be, but I 'quite rightly' pass for an unbeliever"— even as we pray, "I believe, help my unbelief."

On Passing for Atheists along with the Early Christians

But there is yet another way that I think any Christian *can* authentically confess to quite rightly pass for an atheist. In fact, I would go so far as to say that every Christian *should* be (mis)taken for an atheist. Now, before the inquisitors begin to build their brush piles and gather their tinder, let me confess that I am speaking of being taken for an atheist in a certain sense and for a particular reason. And on this point, I take my cue from the reputation of the early Christians within the Roman Empire. This may come as a surprise, but the early Christians were commonly referred to

17. My paraphrase. The NIV translation reads, "Not that I have already obtained all this, or have already been made perfect, but I press on to take hold of that for which Christ Jesus took hold of me."

18. Caputo, *Philosophy and Theology*, 63.

as "atheists." And I would argue that there are important insights to be gleaned from this little known fact of Christian history, not only for the contemporary dialogue between confessing Christians and confessing atheists, but also for our reflection on the Christian community's social, political, and economic practice (or way of life) and our diagnosis of and resistance to the idols of our time.

Clearly, the way to begin to trace the outlines of early Christianity is through an examination of the Scriptures. However, the various accounts of Christians by those outside the Christian community are also beneficial in this endeavor. For example, between AD 106 and AD 114, when Pliny the Younger was governor of Bithynia (a state in Asia Minor), he encountered the problem of having large numbers of people brought before him on charges of being Christian. Not knowing what to do about this, as it would still be another ten years or so until the rules for the persecution of Christians would be standardized throughout the empire, Pliny the Younger wrote a letter to Emperor Trajan explaining his preliminary course of action and asking for further guidance:

> I considered that I should dismiss any who denied that they were or ever had been Christians when they had repeated after me a formula of invocation to the gods and had made offerings of wine and incense to your statue . . . and furthermore had reviled the name of Christ.[19]

Pliny also included an account of the characteristics of these early Christians gathered from his observations:

> They had met regularly before dawn on a fixed day to chant verses alternatively amongst themselves in honor of Christ as if to a god, and also to bind themselves by oath, not for any criminal purpose, but to abstain from theft, robbery, and adultery, to commit no breach of trust and not to deny a deposit when called upon to restore it. After this ceremony it had been their custom to disperse and reassemble later to take food of an ordinary, harmless, kind; but they had in fact given up this practice since my edict, issued on your [i.e., Trajan's] instructions, which banned all political societies. This made me decide that it was all the more necessary to extract the truth by torture from two slave-women, whom they

---

19. Pliny *Letters* 10.96; cited in Wright, *New Testament and the People of God*, 349. Pliny the Younger was the nephew of the naturalist Pliny the Elder, who died while observing the eruption of Mount Vesuvius in AD 79.

call deaconesses. I found nothing but a degenerate sort of cult carried out to extravagant lengths.[20]

As Pliny's letter to Trajan reveals, the fundamental charge leveled against the Christians was their refusal to pray to the Roman deities and participate in emperor worship.

The account of the martyrdom of Polycarp, a bishop of Smyrna and disciple of the Apostle John who was executed around AD 155, provides an explicit link between the early Christians' refusal to participate in standard forms of emperor worship and their designation as atheists:

> There was a great uproar of those who heard that Polycarp had been arrested. Therefore when he was brought forward the Pro-Consul asked him if he were Polycarp, and when he admitted it he tried to persuade him to deny [his Christian faith], saying: "Respect your age," and so forth, as they are accustomed to say: "Swear by the genius [or personified deity] of Caesar, repent, and say: 'Away with the Atheists.'"[21]

As the account of Polycarp's martyrdom demonstrates, Christians were persecuted and killed because their ultimate allegiance was to Jesus rather than Caesar. Put simply, to proclaim that Jesus is Lord was to simultaneously proclaim that Caesar was not, which was tantamount both to treason and blasphemy within the empire. It is for this reason that the early Christians were referred to as atheists, that is, they were atheistic with respect to the official religion of the Roman Empire and all that it entailed.

Moreover, if "logic" concerns "what follows" (in this case, what follows from one's ultimate allegiance or commitment), then we can say that the early Christians' lifestyle ran counter to the imperial logic, the lifestyle consistent with emperor worship and imperial expectation. Refusing to pay homage to Caesar as "the son of god" was enough to warrant persecution in itself, but it was the Christians' different understanding of what it meant to be human and the way that this was expressed in their

---

20. Ibid. Notice the reference to the practice, which was quite progressive for its day, of giving women ("slave-women," no less) prominent roles of leadership within the congregational life of churches.

21. Justin Martyr *Martyrdom of Polycarp* 9.1–3; cited in Wright, *New Testament*, 347; italics added.

communal life that unnerved the guardians of empire about the Christians to the extent that they persecuted them so harshly.

Now, it is important to note just what the Christians were actually doing that warranted their designation as a degenerate atheistic cult. It is not that they exposed their children to the practice of pederasty and participated in sexual orgies in the context of cultic worship (as the Romans did). It is not that they attempted to overthrow the government through violent revolution (as the Zealots did). It is not that they defecated on public sidewalks and committed suicide as a form of public protest (as the Cynics did). And it is not that they restricted their benevolence to their families and ethnic communities (as was standard practice throughout the empire). Rather, as Aristides notes:

> Their oppressors they appease and make them their friends; they do good to their enemies. . . . they love one another, and from widows they do not turn away their esteem; and they deliver the orphan from him who treats him harshly. And he, who has, gives to him who has not, without boasting. And when they see a stranger, they take him in to their homes and rejoice over him as a very brother; for they do not call them brethren after the flesh, but brethren after the spirit and of God. And whenever one of their poor passes from the world, each one of them according to his ability gives heed to him and carefully sees to his burial.[22]

The early Christians were accused of being an atheistic cult not because they were doing things that we would recognize today as degenerate—quite the opposite—but because their total way of life, interpersonally, communally, and within society at large, was out of step with the *mores* (from where we get the term "morality") or cultural conventions of their day. For the early Christians, to keep covenant with the God of Jesus Christ meant being "immoral" with respect to the logic of the empire and the imperial way of life.

One of the fascinating features of early Christianity is that within a few decades after the crucifixion of its founding figure at the hands of the Romans, the early Christians had managed to distinguish their communal life and public practice—what I would refer to collectively as their "way" (of life)—from every other community in the Roman Empire.[23] Aristides'

22. Aristides *Apology* 15; cited in Wright, *New Testament*, 363.

23. For this reason, Christianity was commonly referred to as the "third way," even as

account could not be said of the Stoics and Cynics, the paganism and the mystery cults of popular Roman religion, or any of the various forms of either Second Temple or Rabbinical Judaism. As the first-century historian and New Testament scholar N. T. Wright argues:

> What we seem to be faced with is the existence of a community which was perceived to be subverting the normal social and cultural life of the empire precisely by its quasi-familial, quasi-ethnic life as a community . . . . It was a new family, a "third race," neither Jew nor Gentile but "in Christ." Its very existence threatened the foundational assumptions of pagan society.[24]

In their total way of life, from their symbolic actions (e.g., refusing to participate in emperor worship) to their social practices (e.g., hospitality that transcended religious, ethnic, and socioeconomic boundaries), the early Christians were challenging the assumptions of empire and embodying a new way of being human that was out of step with the imperial logic. This is the most plausible explanation for why the early Christians faced such intense persecution and why they were commonly referred to as atheists within the Roman Empire. As Wright suggests, "What evokes persecution is precisely that which challenges a worldview, that which up-ends a symbolic universe."[25]

If Christians today are to "quite rightly" pass for atheists in the sense that this term was applied to the early Christians, as I believe all Christians should, then we must begin by asking two related questions: What are the analogies to Roman emperor worship in our own historical moment? And what does it mean to be truly human?

With regard to the first question, in order to establish the contemporary analogies to Roman emperor worship, we must analyze the reigning "gods of our age," those ideologies that demand our ultimate allegiance, and denounce them in sacrilegious fashion (indeed, in atheistic fashion)

---

they commonly referred to themselves as "people of the way." I find quite helpful the idea that religions are pretheoretical and holistic "ways of life" that are not ultimately reducible to the "theories of life" (worldviews) or "theories of God" (theologies) which pertain to them. For more on the notion that human beings are inescapably religious creatures and that religion encompasses and expresses itself in all of life—that "life is religion," see Runner, *Relation of the Bible to Learning*; and Vander Goot, *Life Is Religion*.

24. Wright, *New Testament*, 450.

25. Ibid., 451.

as the idols of our time. To begin this process of ideological identification and critique, I suggest that we take a second look at the isms that are characteristic of the American way of life. Isms, in the sense that I will develop as "good things gone bad," are revelatory of the idolatrous tendencies of a society as a whole. In this sense, isms get at the idols that we all live in witting and unwitting obedience to, whether we come from a red state or a blue state, or consider ourselves liberals or conservatives. In other words, when it comes to ideology, or what we might think of as societal idolatry, left, right, or center, we all worship at the same altar.

The identification of the idols of our time is serious business, and with limited space for argumentation, the best I can do is to refer to the work of those I am drawing upon as I suggest that any diagnosis of the most problematic isms of our day and age should include, at minimum, *nationalism* (the pursuit of national interest and national security at any cost), *technologism* (the pursuit of scientific discovery and technological advancement at any cost), and *economism* (the pursuit of profit and economic expansion at any cost).[26] Now, I do not mean to imply that these pursuits are bad in and of themselves. It is, rather, their pursuit at any cost, which gives them their god-like status, that I am specifically critiquing. When properly related to other creaturely priorities, national identity and national security, scientific discovery and technological progress, and capital growth and economic profit will most likely be a part of any good world that we can imagine. However, when these creaturely phenomena are turned into isms, when they are absolutized and treated as objects of ultimate and unqualified allegiance that we obey at any cost, they stop serving life in its richest and most comprehensive sense and instead become agents of death.

Having said this, we would do well to pause and reflect upon the kind of world these gods have bestowed on us, or I should say, the kind of world we have created in our submission to them—a world characterized by escalating violence and the rise of the military industrial machine, human alienation from nature and vast environmental degradation, the threat of nuclear destruction and biological weaponry, the commodification of

26. My diagnosis of the idols of our time is very much indebted to Walsh and Middleton, *Transforming Vision*; Goudzwaard et al., *Hope in Troubled Times*; and McLaren, *Everything Must Change*.

reality where people become reduced to things in a market where every thing has a price, and a rapidly widening gap between the world's rich and the world's poor—and ask ourselves whether the gods of our age are as benevolent as we have taken them to be, and if they are truly worthy of our service.

With regard to the second question, we must begin to explore new ways of being human that run counter to current imperial expectation— the conventional wisdom determined for us by the gods of our age—and that are instead animated by the biblical vision of a world characterized by justice, solidarity, resourcefulness, and the full flourishing of all God's creatures, both human and non-human. I should say that while I am specifically addressing the way in which a Christian can "pass for an atheist" by denouncing contemporary ideologies, I also assume that Christians have much to learn from people who explicitly identify themselves as atheists, or those who I would call "confessing atheists."

My partner and I are close friends with a couple that profess to be atheists. They are very good people who love justice and care deeply about the world, and we have learned much about how to live more creatively and compassionately through our friendship with them. From this experience I can say that Christians would do well to extend the dialogue beyond familiar borders and listen to as many people as possible in their attempt to discern what it means to live well as human beings in a complex world. This is not just a specifically Christian question, but a very human question, and though centuries of Christian reflection certainly do provide us with a plethora of insights and resources to bring to the table, perhaps we should focus more on hosting hospitable conversations where wisdom can be shared freely rather than attempting to provide the answer ourselves. What it means to be fully and truly human in our time always comes to us as an open question, and in a very important sense, in spite of (and yet without wanting to flatten out) our very real religious differences, we really are all in it together when it comes to crafting a more just and peaceable future.[27]

27. For an example of a mutually illuminating dialogue between a Marxist atheist and a Calvinist Christian that is both respectful of very real religious differences and open to a common search, see Nielsen and Hart, *Search for Community in a Withering Tradition*. It is significant that in his exaugural address as a professor of systematic philosophy at the Institute for Christian Studies, Hart says of Nielsen, "You are an atheist in whom God shows me how to love and do justice to our neighbor, you came [to the exaugural]

I am convinced that any person or community that begins to take these questions to heart will begin to feel the pressure, if not the outright persecution, of the powers that be, those who stand to gain the most from keeping things exactly as they are and reducing life to more of the same.[28] "Away with the Atheists," they will say, as they did with the Christian Bishop Polycarp, of all those who refuse to bend the knee and pay homage to the gods of nationalism, technologism, and economism, to name a few from the contemporary pantheon.[29] And it is in this sense, after a rigorous critique of the idols and ideologies of our time and a reimagining of what it means to live truly human and humane lives, that every Christian should "quite rightly pass for an atheist."

In(con)clusion

Now, for those still suffering from a case of classification fever, I will offer a subtle and suggestive Christian credo of my own:

Am I an atheist? Well, if that means one who no longer desires God and testifies to the reality of God in my life, and one who has given up on the hope of the name of God and the naming of God being significant for human life, then, no, I am not an atheist. But if that means one who is

because you care" (Hart, "Spirit of God").

28. Dr. Martin Luther King Jr. and Nelson Mandela are powerful examples of people who challenged the ideologies of their day to such an extent that the powers that be could no longer tolerate their existence. I would interpret the immediate historical reasons, as well as the starting point for discerning the theological meaning, for Jesus's imprisonment and crucifixion in a similar fashion. We must remember that crucifixion was the form of death reserved for troublemakers within the Roman Empire. Thus, I would interpret the Sermon on the Mount as Jesus's doubly revolutionary articulation of a new way of life to his followers, a way of making holy trouble in the world in the name of love.

29. As I mentioned previously, nationalism, technologism, and economism are my suggestions of a good place to start for identifying the idols of our time. Walsh and Middleton identify the "gods of our age" as "scientism," "technicism," and "economism," which they refer to together as the "unholy trinity." Goudzwaard and colleagues cite three "contemporary ideologies": "unleashed identity," "unshackled material progress and prosperity," and "guaranteed security." And McLaren speaks in terms of an ideological "suicide machine" that has resulted in four "global crises": the "prosperity crisis" (which includes the "ecological crisis"), the "equity crisis," the "security crisis," and the "spirituality crisis." I am very much indebted to these authors' analyses and proposals, and I heartily recommend them, particularly for readers looking for a more detailed, robust account of a Christian social vision and practice than I offer in this essay.

suspicious of the gods of our age (as the idols of our time), and sensitive to the way in which our submission to them leads to injustice and makes life on earth a living hell for far too many far too much of the time, then, yes, I quite rightly pass for an atheist.

Am I a theist? Well, if that means feeling the need to subscribe to the theological doctrines and moral conventions that go by the name of "orthodoxy," and if historically any theism, particularly classical theism, has always been some form of deism (the belief in a distant, dispassionate, and authoritarian supreme being[30]), then, no, I am not a theist. But if it refers to a wholehearted allegiance to God and God's good creation, and if this translates into a desire for God that is simultaneously a desire for justice and a love of God that is simultaneously a love of neighbor,[31] then, yes, I quite rightly pass for a theist.

30. Let me reiterate my concern that the category of theism always smuggles in some form of deism. Deism has its origins in Epicurean notions of the divine, and it comes to its fullest expression in the popular eighteenth-century notion of God as the watchmaker who fashioned creation, wound it up, and left it alone, that is, except for the occasional miraculous supernatural interruption of the laws of nature. Although someone who is familiar with the Scriptures will realize that this is a very different perception of God than the covenanting God of Abraham, Isaac, Jacob, and Jesus, the majority of Christian academic and popular theology that goes by the name of "biblical theism" is (sadly, in my estimation) little more than deism with a biblical veneer. For two helpful discussions of the deistic streak in Christian theology and the beginnings of what I refer to as a more "covenantal" way of understanding the God/world relation, see Robinson, "End of Theism?" and Wright, "God."

31. This notion of "a desire for God that is simultaneously a desire for justice, and a love of God that is simultaneously a love of neighbor" is a natural way to speak about God and creation from within a covenantal perspective—one that assumes that the God of whom we speak is always the God-of-creation and that the creation of which we speak is always the creation-of-God. From within such a perspective it would never be appropriate to pit God (and the love of God) against creation (and the love of creation). Covenantally, by definition, to love the God of creation is to love the creation of God, and to love the creation of God, is to love the God of creation. I take this to be what Dietrich Bonhoeffer was getting at in his *Ethics* when he said that to be truly Christian is to love God and the world in a single unity. I also take this to both echo and address one of the most persistent critiques of Christianity by secular people and confessing atheists alike— the notion that Christians are so heavenly minded that they are of no earthly good. From a covenantal perspective, heavenly mindedness and earthly mindedness would not be understood as mutually exclusive (as they are in both atheism and theism), but rather as mutually intensive or intensifying. This is one way that I see the earthly minded atheistic critique of "heavenly minded" theism as providing, perhaps providentially so, the opportunity for Christian theology to move beyond theism/deism to something more

As you can see, like Augustine, I am truly a question to myself. But at least I am in good company![32]

---

covenantal, and thus, to a spirituality that is both grounded in the earth—as the creational gifts of God, we are called to extend in faith—and open to the heavens—as the creational promises of God, we are called to anticipate in hope. For more on the significance of the heaven/earth relationship for a covenantal spirituality, see Ansell, "It's About Time."

32. I wish to thank Craig Stanley and Del Stanley for their helpful comments on earlier drafts of this essay, as well as my partner, Julie Parker Stanley, for her invaluable editorial assistance. This essay was conceived in the context of conversations about the kind of people we felt God calling us to be(come) as we prepared for the birth of our first child. We therefore dedicate this essay to our daughter, Caedance Parker Stanley, in the hope that "the woman will overcome the warrior" (Jer 31:22).

4

On What Could Quite Rightly Pass for a Fetish

Ben Suriano

Jon Stanley's provocative piece in the preceding chapter, "Why Every Christian Should 'Quite Rightly Pass for an Atheist,'"[1] is notable for the way it facilitates a move beyond the reductionistic tendencies of rigid categorization as well as for the ways it begins to identify and resist the gods of our age. In these pursuits, Stanley also seeks to move beyond the vulgar terms of dogmatic atheisms and theisms alike. In the first part of his essay, Stanley draws heavily upon Derridean insights, especially surrounding Derrida's own claim that he could "quite rightly pass for an atheist." Stanley appeals to Derrida's phrase because of the ambivalence of its adverbial modifying clause, "quite rightly," which supposedly resists any hard and fast classification. He emphasizes this phrase to suggest that Christians, along with Derrida, cannot be categorically pinned down as strict theists because they both quite rightly pass for atheists while also not quite passing for atheists. This exploration of Derrida's thought serves as a *propaedeutic* for launching into cultural criticism that attempts to break with "classification fever." For Stanley, classification fever denotes an obsessive drive to categorize and reduce everything to rigidly set terms, a fever that has become a massive contagion within our culture in that it leads to domination through naming the other.

Stanley then, in the second part of his essay, implicitly extends the Derridean motif more deeply into the realm of cultural criticism by

---

1. Stanley's piece is a well-written, accessible conversation-starter, and my own piece has benefited greatly from extensive conversations with Stanley about the issues covered in these essays. I am also indebted to Dan Rhodes, another colleague and friend at *The Other Journal*.

drawing on the example of early Christians who were deemed atheists in a certain sense within the Roman Empire because they did not bow to Caesar. He insightfully illustrates some of the subversive modes of practice of early Christians against the imperial logic of Rome, practices that won them the charge of atheism. Moreover, he suggests that we, as contemporary Christians, should also "authentically confess" to quite rightly passing for atheists in the qualified sense of the early Christians as we pursue similar ways of identifying and resisting the gods of our age. Stanley passionately urges us in this undertaking: "What are the analogies to Roman emperor worship in our own historical moment? . . . we must analyze the reigning 'gods of our age,' those ideologies that demand our ultimate allegiance, and denounce them in sacrilegious fashion (indeed, in atheistic fashion) as the idols of our time" (20).

Reclaiming something of the subversive core of Christianity in order to more radically challenge and transform our dominant social ideologies is of utmost importance for Christians today. Indeed, Stanley has done us a great favor in passionately articulating this urgent need, and I therefore stand with him in pursuing these concerns.

Yet I believe that such concerns could be more fruitfully pursued without an appeal to atheism or Derrida. I believe that Stanley obscures some of his best insights about the radicality of Christianity by placing too much emphasis on how Christians "quite rightly pass for atheists" and not enough emphasis on how they more significantly do not quite pass for atheists.

I concur with Stanley with regard to the basic thrust of his piece, but I want to claim that here and now, in our historical moment, it is not appropriate to pass for an atheist, not even with Derrida and the application of his ambivalent modifying clause. Such an appeal seems to confuse the urgent matter of determining how Christians should best identify classificatory fever and transform the gods of our age. For what if our current analogies to the Roman imperial logic and its pantheon reside in a deeply problematic form of modern atheism in which even Derrida is complicit? If this is true, then appealing to atheism or quite rightly passing for an atheist in our historical situation is misguided.

There is a common reading of the history of modern Western atheism as a progressive movement of sober negation, as a way of entering more nakedly and freely into the cold hard reality of life without illusions and myths. Such a reading tends to hold an inflated sense of the critical value of modern atheism, as if at its base it were the dangerously sub-versive yet honest and helpful suspicion of stilted conventions and their idols. This popular valorization chooses to ignore that the predominant form of modern atheism is deeply dependent upon and perpetuates an ideological, and therein idolatrous, construction—one that is itself not a progressive coming-of-age or a sobering up, but rather the preservation and refinement of a pagan trajectory of power seeking.

This common reading of modern atheism needs to be more acutely challenged as we seek to identify and transform the ruling ideologies of our age. That is to say, I am moving forward with the critical task that Stanley has set forth of "analyz[ing] the reigning 'gods of our age', those ideologies that demand our ultimate allegiance, and denounce them in sacrilegious fashion" (20). But unlike Stanley, I will not suggest that this task is done in a qualified "atheistic fashion" because modern atheism itself must be analyzed and highlighted as preserving the gods of our age. In other words, I will argue that in denouncing contemporary ideologies and idolatries a Christian should not pass for an atheist, just as the early Christians did not in any real sense pass for atheists. This is because an alternative reading of the main form of modern atheism shows that it carries an ontological thread in common with the assumptions behind the Roman imperial logic—an ontology of bare power that underwrites the gods of the new imperial logic of the liberal nation-state and its late-capitalist market system. Thus, in resisting this modern imperial logic, as Christians we must instead quite rightly pass for Christians by emphasiz-ing the difference of Christianity all the way down to its ontological core.

I am emphasizing this ontological[2] analysis of modern atheism be-cause one must search out the ontological foundations of the position or worldview that one is engaging if one is to deepen its analysis and begin any process of contextualization. Here I will work in complement with, while deepening, the analysis that Stanley has begun, as such an analysis of ontologies was beyond the limited scope of his introductory endeavor. Moreover, an analysis of Derrida's ontology will reveal that he is com-plicit with the entrenched atheistic ontology of the modern imperial logic to such a degree that even his modifying clause is unable to salvage any

2. I am referring to *ontology* in this essay as primarily that modern branch of meta-physics that discourses on the ultimate reality beyond physics; more specifically, ontology studies being, the very ground and nature of reality, and designates those basic assump-tions about reality that make a position or project intelligible and legitimate.

subversive value to passing for an atheist. Indeed, Derrida's continuation of this ontological trajectory could be said to quite rightly pass for a fetish, as I will show.

Foundational Atheistic Assumptions and the Imperial Logic of Rome

Although early Christians rejected the gods of the Roman pantheon, gods who were attached to causal forces and caught up in the contest of blood and soil and violence, the early Christians only did so by way of their allegiance to a peculiar God—something of which the Romans were well aware.[3] The Christian God was peculiar because this God transcended the violent agon of deities (in antiquity *agon* designated a contest or struggle) by being utterly beyond, while at the same time taking on blood and soil in order to endure all violence in the Incarnation. The Incarnation showed another way of being, a way that participates in the plenitude of an eternal love and exceeds this order of violence, revealing it as false and temporary. This is not to say that early Christians viewed the violence of their world as unreal, for although they believed it to be false in a metaphysical sense, they nevertheless understood this agon to be a present and historical reality that was entrenched deep within the structure of human life thus making it appear to be the undeniable way things are.[4]

For the Romans, however, this order of power and violent competition was indeed the way that things were, even down to their metaphysical base. They predominantly held to a view of reality that understood the very being of the world as a disordered melee of conflicting forces, which necessitated appeals to powerful deities who used counterviolence to stay chaos and impose order upon it. Here we have the pagan idea that order is only won through continual conquest or domination within the agon of chaotic forces. Hence, the gods were continually at war. And here the

3. Of course, the precedent for resisting the Roman pantheon was already set by the Jews and their faith in God as the fullness of being, the transcendent I AM beyond the immanent competition of power. I am thankful to Steve Long for emphasizing this in our various conversations.

4. That is, more precisely, evil was false because it was not metaphysically real as it was an inexplicable privation of the good. And yet it is a very present historical reality in our postlapsarian times. So evil is a pervasive historical reality in our postlapsarian times and is therefore not an illusion, but at the same time, as an inexplicable privation of good, it has no inherent purchase on ultimate reality (no metaphysical reality).

imperial logic operates by way of an appeal to metaphysical violence as the way things are, even at the highest level of existence, to legitimate the sovereignty of state power as that sole counterforce that is able to maintain divine favor so as to control and regulate the agon. Justified coercion was then touted as the only way to prevent pandemonium and maintain imperial self-possession.[5]

This predominant Roman metaphysical assumption about reality therefore included a divine realm beyond physical forces, but this assumption is more appropriately understood as a divine realm working in extension with competing physical forces. That is, competing physical forces were the result of competing deities, and therefore, violent competition was just as prevalent at the physical level as at the metaphysical level. Thus, while the Roman assumption about metaphysical reality ostensibly inscribed the physical order within a divine order, everything was nevertheless inscribed within a greater agonistic whole of what could only be the totalized sphere of immanent power and violence. At base, then, their understanding of reality ultimately assumed an immanent enclosure with no reference to something transcending the violent competition between order and disorder, which implicated everything from the gods to basic elements. As I will illustrate later, modern ontology continues this assumption about reality as a totally enclosed arena of force, yet it carries it forward in a more blatantly reductionistic direction that makes no apparent attempt to inscribe reality within a divine, metaphysical order beyond physics.

Deities within the Roman pantheon therefore corresponded merely to valorized immanent forces of conquest and order, and they were organized in such a way so as to buttress the legitimacy and divinity of Caesar's absolute power. Christians, by virtue of their unique God, were thus an absolute befuddlement to the Romans and their nationalistic theology of power. How could a god not be another power broker? How could this sect of people known as Christians deny the existence of what was commonly accepted as the violent agon of the gods?

All would have been well in the Roman Empire had the Christians resigned to this metaphysic of the violent agon, an agon in which Caesar

---

5. For an elaboration and juxtaposition of the two different ontological frameworks between pagan Rome and Christianity as well as an exegesis of the hidden continuity between pagan and modern worldviews see Milbank, *Theology and Social Theory*, ch. 12.

was sovereign, and lowered the status of their peculiar god to that of just another private household deity in subjection to the state religion. But this allegiance was not possible; the eternal love shown in Christ provided a radically different understanding of metaphysical reality. Following Christ meant believing that the being of the world was and is a free gift flowing from God's goodness where the plenitude of eternal love remains prior to any competition between order and disorder. And this different understanding of reality brought forth a different vision of communal flourishing by way of practicing the open, gratuitous sharing of this gift of love with others rather than the exclusionary pursuit of power over others. This difference in metaphysics and its social outworking, therefore, inevitably exposed any attempt to absolutize the realm of violence and conflict as nothing more than the arbitrary tale told by the *libido dominandi* to justify the use of excessive force in the pursuit of *dominium* for its own sake.[6]

Here Stanley is right to point out, along with N. T. Wright, that the Christian way of being cuts straight to the heart of this ancient view of the world, challenging the very foundations of pagan society and the entire symbolic universe of the Roman imperial project. Yet this is only because the Roman and Christian worldviews assume something vastly different about reality at its metaphysical and, therein, ontological depth. Furthermore, to reiterate Stanley's analysis but with more emphasis on the metaphysical differences, it is because this challenge was directed all the way down to the very core of what underwrote the legitimacy of the imperial logic and its state apparatuses of control that we can make sense of why it provoked such an intense persecution of Christians, who were often charged as "atheists," a grave indictment at the time.

As Stanley elaborates in his essay, a notable example of this Christian indictment on charges of atheism is found in the legend of Polycarp's martyrdom. It must be emphasized, however, that the charge of "atheism" did not mean that the Romans believed the Christians to be without a God. Rather, the charge implied that Christians were without loyalty to the divinity of Caesar and the state-sponsored religion, as Stanley has duly noted. The Romans knew Christians worshipped a God that was inassimilable to and incommensurable with their imperial project. This burgeoning little sect, which inhibited the pursuit of power by not

---

6. See Augustine *City of God*, preface.

cooperating with the imperial cult, began to pose a national security threat that required the harshest treatment. And the charge of atheism was ultimately a trumped-up one in order to vilify this sect, framing it as an uncivilized, treacherous alien within, a dangerous threat that required an exceptional use of violence to purge it and reinforce imperial identity.[7]

This charge of atheism was trumped-up not only to vilify a perceived threat and justify exceptional violence but also, in bolstering the hallowed aura of imperial sovereignty, to further conceal the debased core of atheistic power-lust behind the allegedly sacred veil of its judicial authority. A full account of Polycarp's trial that gives not merely the accusations leveled against him but also, more significantly, his response to these accusations (an exchange Stanley leaves out) shows that Polycarp was fully aware of this subterfuge; he not only rejected the charge of atheism, but he also rejected the judicial authority issuing such an indictment by throwing the charge back upon the Roman audience, shaking his fist at them and proclaiming, "Away with the atheists."[8] The story, therefore, does not stop with Polycarp quite rightly passing for an atheist in any meaningful sense, for by maintaining his allegiance to Christ, he saw through the pseudo-sacred imperial spectacle, charging that it was this Roman order instead that quite rightly passed for a fundamentally atheistic ideology. In fact, many of the early Christians such as Clement of Alexandria, Origen, and Tertullian refuted the charge of atheism by seeking to explicitly expose the real atheistic core of their pagan accusers.[9]

Resisting the gods of the age, then, meant rightly passing for a Christian. A metaphysics that emphasized a radically different source for the very being of things, which in no significant way was atheistic, made possible the cultivation of new modes of practice, which were also in no significant way atheistic, and that allowed one to see through the supposedly sacred, imperial veil to its truly atheistic core. And although this fundamentally atheistic aspect was only implicit in the Roman order, obliquely translated and expressed in cultural-religious codes surrounding the state pantheon, it was nevertheless an essential element in reducing reality to agonistic power so as to maintain the legitimacy and aura of imperial sovereignty. To reiterate, then, what rightly passed for atheism

7. See Thompson, "Martyrdom of Polycarp."

8. *Martyrdom of St. Polycarp*, 94.

9. See Bremmer, "Atheism in Antiquity."

was the limiting of metaphysical reality, in the interest of state power, to an immanent arena of conflict. Thus, in this context, atheism was not a subversive way of calling into question the pantheon supporting the imperial project but was itself a hidden foundational assumption that made imperial power possible.

Atheistic Ontology and the Imperial Logic of the Modern West

Modern atheism, in its various forms, should be seen as more in line with this implicitly atheistic, pagan metaphysic of violent force and its outworkings in imperial apparatuses of control rather than as any kind of continuation of the spirit within the radically subversive metaphysic and ethos of the Christian movement.[10] Whereas Christianity, in a creational and incarnational register, increasingly formed new ways of seeing the nature of reality as fundamentally a gift participating in the infinite love of God, the modern world opened by, *inter alia*, bracketing out and soon ridding itself entirely of this theological and metaphysical assumption in order to focus exclusively on a bare ontology of being in its supposed nakedness. That is, the predominant ontologies of modernity reduced reality to a bare given of efficient causality rather than a gift given always anew from an exceeding source—a move which in effect unhooked ontology from any more substantive metaphysic, especially in any theological form. Although various forms of this ontological trajectory were influenced by and remained within certain Christian contexts (of nominalist and voluntarist tendencies), these modernist ontologies were nevertheless implicitly atheistic, as the being of the world was understood to be an indifferent field of brute force that was able to be grasped without any reference to a divine order. Atheism in its predominant modern form is the continuation of this reductionistic trajectory in a more explicitly immanent manner. This reductionistic direction more thoroughly seals off the realm of causal forces from communicating anything other than their measurable, objectifiable surface play of force in order to make this realm

10. Granted, modern atheism can be attributed to a complex milieu of influences, and indeed, aspects of the Judeo-Christian movement can be seen, to a certain degree, as contributing to its specific rise and form. But where this is the case, it can also be argued that such occurred when radical aspects of the Judeo-Christian perspective were forgotten and perversely forged into an ontology that was complicit with an understanding of reality as mere conflicting forces.

readily available for the imperious survey of autonomous thought. And this atheistic move toward a tightly sealed enclosure is the underpinning for the more thoroughgoing escalation of "classification fever" of which Stanley speaks.[11]

Although modern atheism may show itself to be ostensibly a break from the more overtly mythical language of the pagan universe, it is nevertheless in continuity in a certain important sense. For while modern atheism claims to be denuding nature of its sacral allure, ridding reality of any anthropomorphic projections, it still, at its base, holds to a variation of the Roman metaphysical assumption that everything is bound to an immanent conflict of violent forces. And as the modern thinker no longer gives these forces divine names, it is the sealed-off sphere of nature itself, within its own immanent power, that is often given the divine attributes of being ultimate, absolute, law-like, and all-powerful. Thus, modern atheism continues to preach a core ontological thread of immanent power and conflict as total, though in a more reduced, bald form; however, this reduced form is not the inevitable result of discovering an unadorned, naked world of force after peeling back the mythical coverings. Instead, modern atheism is just another construct that privileges a certain assignment of exalted attributes within the immanent realm, though in the more austere, minimalist terms of a supposedly disenchanted natural order.[12]

Moreover, this atheistic ontology of blind power has become increasingly accepted and internalized in our world, as if it were the natural, unquestioned view of reality. As this atheistic ontological assumption is taken for granted, it entrenches itself deep within the collective imagination, shaping the structural assumptions of modern Western social,

11. I am merely highlighting a few of the essential aspects of the dominant ontological assumptions of modernity and by no means claiming that modernity is only this. Moreover, in tracing a certain atheistic trajectory, I am not claiming that atheism is only expressed in this form—again, we are only looking at one of its main ontological characteristics, which has deeply influenced the rise of the secular West and therein allows the more popular current atheistic expressions. Nor am I saying that modernity is all bad, but I am rather emphasizing some of its egregious parts that have exerted a massive influence in the world. Nor am I claiming that there is no longer any religious aspect to the structuring of modern society, rather that although this aspect still lingers in various forms, it has increasingly been pushed out of the picture at the ontological level.

12. This contingent, constructed character is becoming more evident in recent scholarship, which is also pointing to the deeply held quasi-spiritual motives and practices surrounding this trajectory. For instance, see Buckley, *At the Origins of Modern Atheism*; and Taylor, *Secular Age*.

political, and economic life. For with no higher causes or substantive ends, there remain only agonistic power relations and the elevation of means to ends. And this atheistic ontology is the predominant animating ground behind the gods of our age; it is the founding ism that conditions all of the other isms that should be emphasized along with Stanley's description of the pantheon of nationalism, militarism, technologism, scientism, and economism. For here, this atheistic ontology ensures that nothing other than the pursuit of abstract power, efficiency, utility, profit, and wealth are allowed to stand as ends guiding the organization of social reality in the modern West. Most notably, with the excising of any metaphysical reality that would make relative the realm of agonistic power, the floodgates have been opened for the pursuit of power to be regulated only by more power, thus legitimating the modern nation-state-building project in its unquestioned sovereignty.[13]

Yet because the efficient accumulation of power through competition is ever more held as the most basic and highest pursuit—above more cumbersome national and ethnic interests—the capitalist market, with its formal mechanisms that indifferently organize, refine, and expand the competition, is apotheosized as the ultimate arena around which to structure social reality. Accordingly, the imperial logic of the modern Western state-building project is now more fully oriented around a neoliberal allegiance to establishing and securing the "free" market.[14] By using its vast networks of bureaucratic mechanisms and military-technological apparatuses, the state polices any threat to the functioning of these market systems, making sure the market regulates and expands itself efficiently in order to provide more opportunities for accumulation.

Organizing social structures around the market arena also requires the state to set in place techniques of discipline and control that shape its own collective body toward this highest goal of market utility. Such techniques of control operate according to the assumption that all beings are able to be comprehensively surveyed and classified primarily as "resources," that is, as potential forces to be managed for the accumulation

13. For an account of how the nation-state project was legitimated through promoting the myth of necessary violence and power, and thereby usurping authority from other spheres of social reality, see Cavanaugh, "Killing for the Telephone Company," esp. 249–51; and Tilly, "War Making and State Making as Organized Crime."

14. The term *neoliberal* designates a worldview that believes that the autonomous self-regulation of the market should ultimately organize all other social reality.

and storing of power. This sense of being is then internalized deep within our collective and individual self-understanding through a diverse array of social scripts, whether directly through entertainment or media discourses, current business models, public policies, or more subtly, through the likes of civil engineering and educational structures. Here it is important to realize that the ethos of modern capitalism is not some sort of hedonistic greed or bacchanalian consumption, but the single-minded, joyless, disciplined pursuit of the accumulation of abstract wealth and *dominium* for its own sake. This pursuit is serious business and demands stringent codes of discipline for the shaping of desire to fit a certain ascetic form of unconditional obedience and ultimate allegiance to the market.

Consequently, what we find is that a world of mere power without God (a-theos) is not one where desire is jovially liberated into heightened possibilities, nor is it a celebration of life where everything is permitted, as it is often advertised. Rather, it is a world set loose only to simultaneously enclose itself within an iron cage of cold instrumental rationality; it is a prison where life is not celebrated with joy and freedom but is effectively and fretfully drained of intrinsic worth and then subsequently commodified (its parody of re-enchantment[15])—everything breaks down to being either a potential threat to or investment for market exchange and, therefore, kept under constant surveillance.[16]

One of the most important techniques of discipline and surveillance in the modern imperial project of market hegemony is to eliminate from substantive religious ends any political or economic significance. This is done through the policing of religion by redefining it as merely a private, inward affair. Religious ends are then relegated to the realm of private household matters, and even there they are only meant to help one personally cope with the rigors of secular, market competition. And this means that religion is to subordinate itself to state regulations and market operations without questioning the assumption that these structures are naturally the best means to negotiate social order and peace in the "real world" of strife. Yet accepting this subordinate position is the same as

15. For an elaboration on commodification as re-enchantment see McCarraher, "Enchantments of Mammon."

16. That this modern world of mere power has caged itself within its own mechanisms of control is not by any means a novel insight but is readily exposed, in different ways, by various thinkers from Max Weber to Theodor Adorno and from Jacques Ellul to Martin Heidegger and Michel Foucault, to name only a few.

accepting the fundamentally atheistic ontology of power. The effect is to eliminate both political and ontological significance from religion, stripping it down to a bourgeois matter of mere intentions or a pragmatic opiate to console market losers. In either case, religion is thus cordoned off to some ethereal inward sphere, while the body and all materiality are appropriated and disciplined according to the business proper within modern politics and economics; religion comforts the soul while sociopolitical structures convert the body into an exchangeable commodity available for market utility. Of course, in this scheme religion is indeed an opiate, but it is an opiate that is packaged and sold by a deeper atheistic ideology, an ideology that is dead set on protecting the status quo.

What rightly passes for an atheistic core runs from the imperial logic of Rome to the imperial logic of the modern West. At its base it is a metaphysic or more minimal ontology that reduces the being of the world, and indeed all of reality, to agonistic power relations, thereby alleging that the highest pursuit is an ordered control and accumulation of power as an end in itself. Moreover, the apparently inescapable character of this ontology of power and violence is appealed to in order to make necessary and hence to justify the use of counterforce by way of absolute state sovereignty and its formal mechanisms of regulation and discipline. The Roman and modern construal of reality as agonistic can also be seen in the founding political myths of each age, myths that portray primal violence as the most basic reality in order to justify further violence: there is the fratricidal story of Romulus and Remus, and there is Hobbes's *Leviathan* with its "war of all against all" as the primal state of nature. The purpose of tracing these metaphysical and ontological threads is to underline the fact that atheism has by and large not grown as a subversive element in the modern world, as if progressing away from the foundational assumptions of pagan society, but rather, atheism can be understood as a conservative element that refines and conserves more purely and ascetically, through greater apparatuses of control, the core of the *libido dominandi.*

Thus, in speaking of resisting the gods of our age, which are the gods of power, a power that is itself primarily shaped and authorized by this atheistic ontology, the phrase "to quite rightly pass for an atheist" can only maintain minimal rhetorical significance if it is employed in a highly ironic tone. Yet I fear that such irony would have to stretch itself too far to be able to overcome the profound status quoism of modern atheism.

Atheistic Ontology and Derrida

An appeal to Derrida cannot move one closer to understanding how to usefully pass for an atheist, especially as it relates to how a Christian might challenge and transform this order. Derrida himself remains complicit with the standing modern order at the level of both ontology and practice. Although Derrida's work at times incisively calls into question some of the most privileged modern mechanisms for imposing order upon the agon of power, he ultimately avoids questioning the agon itself.[17]

For Derrida, being is the oppositional conflict between binaries, but what is more real than even this duel of forces is the difference between them. That is, the binary oppositions (such as order and disorder, rational and irrational, presence and absence, identity and difference, and so on) vie for position and importance, yet what is more important is the differing space and temporal deferment—or *différance*, as Derrida coins it—in between: a *khora* that is not one of the oppositions but that allows them to stand out distinctively against one another in the first place. That is to say, in the conflict of binaries one term usually masquerades as being more real, as beyond contamination by these differential relations, and thereby conquers the other. But Derrida shows through his elaboration of *différance* that neither term in the binary truly conquers the other because both need the other in order to stand out, and that both are, in fact, constituted at their foundation by this continual supplementation of difference.[18] Thus, no term is beyond the other, but both are equally inscribed within the more primordial differential space between, that "bottomless chessboard upon which being is put into play."[19] Therefore, whereas the pagan and modern ontologies of power accept the agon of conflicting dualities yet privilege an allegedly justified violent order over disorder, Derrida privileges the bottomlessness of the chessboard duel in

17. For some of his best work in deconstructing the modern god of transcendental subjectivity, see Derrida, *Speech and Phenomena*. For other elaborations on how Derrida reifies violence, see Milbank, *Theology and Social Theory*; and Dews, *Logics of Disintegration*.

18. For *différance* and "supplementarity," see Derrida's *Margins of Philosophy*; but also his *Of Grammatology* and *Writing and Difference*. For *khora* see Derrida, "Khora," where he calls *différance* the *khora*, that empty receptacle in Plato's *Timaeus*, which describes again a sense of indescribable emptiness or bottomlessness at base.

19. Derrida, *Margins of Philosophy*, 22.

order to call out the essential arbitrariness of privileging any one term over the other.

Derrida's philosophy of *différance* aims to liberate beings from their domination within the sovereign order. His work argues that in light of the bottomlessness of the chessboard, a bottomlessness that is impervious to imperial logic, beings are no longer ontologically positioned as pawns because there are no hierarchically set power schemes. Yet in several fundamental ways, the agonism only gets exacerbated.

The idea of bottomlessness might expose any stable order or victory as a forgery, but it also therein enthrones the endlessness of the conflict as absolute, assuming a veritably endless "war of all against all." What we have in the bottomless chessboard of *différance* is nothing more than an absolutization of the infinite regress involved in the endless spacing between finite oppositions implying that the opposition itself will always be in play—again, a more thorough reduction to immanence and another perpetuation of the myth, now in even more austere terms, that the immanent sphere of conflicting power is all there is. So for Derrida, what is most real, then, is the abyss of *différance*, or the bottomless aspect of the chessboard, which is to say that it is an ultimate transcendental emptiness out of which everything impossibly, endlessly, and agonistically emerges and in relation to which nothing has a more or less significant relationship.[20]

Consequently, and contrary to what Derrida would have us believe, this perspective operates within the market ontology; it levels reality down to a play of fungible things and by no means honors the unique singularity of beings. For in relation to an ultimate indifferent emptiness, everything is classified at its base by an essential equivalence, with no thing expressing a greater degree of goodness or beauty or truth than the next thing, thereby ensuring that it is only through subjective imposition—that is, by way now of a thing's commodified form and exchange value—that any worth whatsoever can be attributed to it. The market all too happily accepts this ontological construal as in line with its own justification and

20. It is transcendental in the sense that it is considered a transcendent condition of possibility for reality. In other words, it is that which allows and conditions things to be at all, but is not a thing itself. That Derrida does consider this bottomless *différance* or *khora* as a transcendental necessity, despite his qualifications about it being only a "quasi-transcendental," is especially seen, among other places, in his handling of *khora* as that "preoriginary, *before* and outside all generation," which is a "necessity" that "precedes" and "carries" philosophy ("Khora," 125–26).

continued sprawl and thus renders the critical, liberative edge of Derrida's deconstruction largely domesticated. For within this Derridean scheme, all we can do is arbitrarily hope that somehow a universal realization of this bottomless abyss will help in chastening our imperial ambitions, mitigating the still inevitable conflict of power. Yet all the while, the new imperial logic of the market spreads increasingly uninhibited over this bottomless frontier, aided by having the last remaining vestiges of any other obstructive metaphysical values removed from the sociopolitical chessboard.

The enthroning of Derrida's abyss is not only in line with the atheistic ontological assumptions we have been highlighting as part of an imperial logic, but it also quite rightly passes over from a possible mode of critical thinking to what could be considered a fetish. With the absolute determined as an ineffable emptiness, entailing also that the agon of violence is total, there is a more thorough acceptance of this ontological scheme as the most basic, unavoidable reality behind all other realities, as if this were an eternal necessity that was off-limits to thought. For as the empty void is held as the transcendental condition of being, somehow conditioning the construction and deconstruction of every reality and yet believed to be itself indeconstructible, it remains the last unquestioned and pseudo-sacred absolute while hiding its own contingent character. We have, then, the more severely entrenched myth of an absolute emptiness fantastically attributing to itself a sovereign value beyond its real worthlessness and contingent nature, and with this false attribution lies the problematic character of the fetish in its self-absorption.

This can be seen especially in Derrida's later ethical and religious writings, where he esteems this sovereign emptiness as somehow, perhaps magically, the grounds for ethical earnestness.[21] If there is an absolute ideal of justice, the gift, or forgiveness for Derrida, it is because these ideals exist completely outside the agonistic economy of power. Yet outside this sphere of conflict, which is supposedly total, they are nothing. For Derrida, however, that they are ineffably empty and impossible is also, paradoxically, the condition of their possibility, for in pursuing such vacuous ideals we are impassioned always for more, and we are thereby kept from falling into the theoretical presumption and practical complacency

21. For Derrida's treatment of justice, see *Acts of Religion*, 228–98; for hospitality, see ibid., 356–420; for forgiveness, see "To Forgive"; and for the gift, see *Given Time* and *Gift of Death*.

that are characteristic of believing we have somehow arrived or accomplished something. The point, apparently, is that our desire is here kept in continual striving as it pursues what will never be attained, and more importantly, this purifies the inner intentions and movements of desire toward an unconditional allegiance to the ideal. The real point, however, is that there is no real, full, plenitudinous ideal of justice, goodness, or love that gives itself to be known and that could draw desire out of itself (what for a Christian would be the real transcendentals, which are supremely revealed in the incarnation of Christ). Rather, there is only the absence of these ideals, a barren condition that aids desire in ascetically refining itself toward an unconditional desire of desire itself, so that ultimately, it is the purified desiring, and not the thing desired, that counts.

In other words, the fetishizing of emptiness comes to the fore in that the emptiness of the ideal is projected as more absolute than the ideal itself by a desire that is exclusively preoccupied with its own bottomless movement. Thus, the mysterious source of ethics here is really the ineluctable emptiness that is found at the heart of the modern subject when it is brought to the confounding breakdown of its own desire for itself and not the fullness of an exceeding source beyond.

Furthermore, this is the debased form of mystery that seems to linger within the Derridean reading of Augustine. Such a reading often omits references to God in elaborating the fact that Augustine speaks of being a mystery to himself. But Augustine's mystery of self occurs because he is put into question by an infinite fullness beyond himself—that is, he knows the God of Christ to be closer to him than he is to himself. This Augustinian mystery, then, contrary to Derridean thought, is certainly not due to some modern epistemological insight about how we have limited knowledge, if any, of ourselves. Such a modern/Derridean insight about the limitations of self-knowledge is oddly expected, somehow on its own, to inspire a respect for the other without any revealed and manifested idea of how love for this other could even take place. With such a vacuous notion of mystery, then, emptiness and absence remain the fetishized occasion by which desire continually and impossibly seeks to engage and purify itself within the endless inner conflict of its own desiring. This is really what Derrida seems to mean, a very important point that Stanley does not always fully clarify when he exhorts us to remain a question to ourselves so as to be open to others. For in this Derridean framework, remaining a question to oneself can only mean living a life that looks more like a "knight of infinite resignation," to use a Kierkegaardian idiom. Such a knight only is ascetically concerned with the limitations and incapacities of his or her own intentions, knowledge, and desiring, rather than the "knight of faith" who continually seeks to trust possible answers that can question and pull us beyond ourselves and toward others.[22]

Ultimately, then, this fetishizing of an absolute emptiness passes for a species of that modern fixation with "erotic perplexity," as William Desmond terms it. Erotic perplexity names the tendency of desire to become exclusively preoccupied, indeed obsessed, with its own lack and yearning, rather than with the compelling reality beyond itself that it yearns after, as is characteristic of, on the other hand, what Desmond calls "agapeic astonishment."[23]

Moreover, this fetishizing of emptiness is also a deeply modern bourgeois move toward the privatization and interiorization of religion. This is continually evidenced in Derrida's later writings on ethics and religion where he uses an unoriginal, modern approach in searching out the abstracted, universal logic behind religious traditions, emptying integral themes of their particular content and assimilating them into a mysticism of empty ideals, in a "religion without religion."[24] Derrida even classifies himself as privately holding to what could quite rightly pass for a conventionally personalized religion of inwardness, what he calls "my religion about which nobody understands anything . . . in my absolved, absolutely private language."[25] But an inward religion of which "nobody understands anything," where there is neither "an eyewitness nor . . . a

22. For Kierkegaard's use of "knight of infinite resignation" and "knight of faith," see *Fear and Trembling*. In my unpublished master's thesis, "Dancing beyond the Rabbi and the Poet," I give a substantial argument for why Derrida is to be understood best within the Kierkegaardian category of infinite resignation rather than Kierkegaard's other categories pertaining to the aesthete or that of faith.

23. See Desmond, *Being and the Between*.

24. See especially *Gift of Death* and *Acts of Religion*, 40–101, particularly 56–57, where Derrida claims that his discourse on religion is established by a "desert abstraction" that "in uprooting the tradition that bears it, in atheologizing it, this abstraction, without denying faith, liberates a universal rationality." And for a good analysis of the more rational, Kantian aspect of Derrida's modern handling of religion, see James K. A. Smith's "Re-Kanting Postmodernism?" and "Determined Violence."

25. Derrida, "Circumfession," 154–55.

voice doing anything other than talking to me without saying anything,"[26] as Derrida states, is nothing other than a more thorough submission of "religion" to the policed and tamed private sphere that is in service to the sovereign market. And when Derrida utters the quip about "quite rightly passing for an atheist" in the same breath that he speaks about his "religion," we then find that the clause's essential ambivalence is born out of and hence deconstructible to a private, endlessly agonistic bout around a fetishized emptiness rather than being inspired by and open to a transcendent, intense reality that calls one beyond the endless war of oppositional terms.[27]

Such a position, then, is in line with the status quo and those who are in power. It is therefore a serious oversight to think that Derrida's philosophy could somehow, even as merely a qualified propaedeutic, move us beyond the classificatory gaze and its vulgar understanding of atheism/ theism or aid us in giving voice to the voiceless masses who are dispossessed and marginalized by this system. Derrida is then neither a saint nor a heretic nor a devilish radical, but rather a very pedestrian modern whose ontology and practice are caught within the ideological assumptions that uphold the imperial logic of the late-capitalist market.

Thus, Derrida's ambivalent modifying clause, "quite rightly," lacks even minimal subversive rhetorical value because its meaning has already been dictated by a fetishized ontological thread that also runs throughout the market hegemony. And if it were to remain within this Derridean register, the question of whether every Christian should also quite rightly pass for an atheist should only be answered with a decisive "not quite."

Conclusion

I have sought to show how atheism is deeply problematic by claiming that both the predominant modern form of atheism and Derrida's variation of atheism have no critical value because these forms are primarily

26. Ibid.

27. Caputo aptly spells out the ground upon which Derrida's ambivalence is here based, as he claims that it is due to the insight that "what we call the 'I' is implicated in a kind of conflict of competing voices that give each other no rest" (*Philosophy and Theology*, 63). Derrida's phrase comes out of this ontology and its fetishized war of desire and unknowing, where nothing moves beyond atheism and theism but rather both continually antagonize one another.

self-enclosing, conservative movements that perpetuate the gods of sheer power. This is not to say, however, that atheism is a single uniform thing that is forever set in stone. But it is to claim that this dominant trajectory of Western atheism, with its insidious imperial logic that runs parallel to the ancient pagan trajectory, is so deeply agonistic and bleak at the level of ontology and so deeply entrenched within the systems of our modern world that it renders any use of or comparison with atheism for Christians much more difficult in our current historical moment. I do not intend to suggest that Stanley would endorse this problematic ontology and its outcome, as indeed his piece recognizes that any use of atheism and Derrida must be limited and restrained. Yet I am trying to push and pull on some of Stanley's best insights, moving them in a different direction by posing an assessment of the predominant form of atheism and Derrida at the ontological level, as a question to his piece—why appeal, even in a limited sense, to a position, no matter how ambivalent or ironical it may be, that is hard-pressed to pass for something other than a contrived radicalization that is still complicit with its vulgar and conventional counterpart? Why not reemphasize with greater development and nuance how a Christian, in resisting classification fever and the reductionistic gods of our age, should rightly continue to pass for a Christian through a way of being that is radically beyond both atheism and theism alike? This would be to claim all of reality as a gift given from beyond itself by God as the transcendent fullness of all that is.

5

Holding On

Luci Shaw

Seven days since the storm
snowed itself out and moved east, and still
the fat clots of white lodge themselves
in the twig forks. How cold holds!
This snow fruit crotched in place
by the black dogwood, snared by
a relentless frost that won't
let go, won't give in, even to the sun.
I fixed it in my camera's eye.

On my dining table, in a wood
bowl, wait the five dried pomegranates
I saved for a friend. Decay has
forgotten them, their red skin
dried to tough brown leather,
the little teeth of sepals crimped
in a crown of sharp kisses that guards
the secret seeds, dark purses
for a blood that will never be spilled.

6

Dam(nation) and the American Prophetic Imagination: An Interview with Charles T. Mathewes

DAN RHODES

The Other Journal (TOJ): You and Chris Nichols have a new book, *Prophesies of Godlessness*, in which you say that "in American history prophesies of godlessness are as American as American godliness itself."[1] Can you help us understand why and how these prophetic calls, which lament the decline of American culture toward atheism or godlessness, have been so rooted in American religious culture and imagination?

Charles Mathewes (CM): I think there are two complicated sources for that, at least two, maybe more.

The first source is the religious heritage of most of the original Europeans who came to this continent, especially in the English colonies, the Puritans, and others as well in the southern colonies. Theirs was a profoundly voluntaristic religion, that is, it was a Christianity which was essentially based around the idea of a free and voluntary assent of the will. When you have a religion based around the idea of a fundamentally contingent affirmation of the will, there is always an anxiety about whether or not you are properly voluntarily affirming your religion. There is always a question surrounding the contingency of the propriety of the faith and the future of the faith. That is one source that's internal to the particular religious traditions out of which the nation emerged.

---

1. Mathewes and Nichols, *Prophesies of Godlessness*, from a pre-published, pre-paginated version.

46

The second source is related to the states themselves. We pointed this out in the introduction to *Prophesies of Godlessness*—there is this wonderful quote by Stanley Cavell in his *Must We Mean What We Say?* where he basically says that before there was England the United Kingdom, there was England, and before there was France the Republic, there was France, but before there was the political constellation of the United States of America, there was no America.[2] So America, in a weird way, is a profoundly contingent nation and feels its contingency in its bones. Think about the way the national anthem ends: it ends with a question—"O, Say does that star-spangled banner yet wave / O'er the land of the free and the home of the brave?" In other words, how does America remain America? And because of this, there has been profound anxiety about the continuity of America. Think about the French; the French I believe right now are on their fifth republic. Can you imagine a *second* American republic? That would be so existentially wrenching for people.

Our notion of America thus seems to be that even while it is very strong, it is in some important ways very brittle, and this seems to promote a kind of concern about the moral future of America, especially because America is historically a civic republic, a polity that relies on a certain sense of moral virtue among its citizens for its sustenance. And Americans have had a hard time, for a long time, working through a picture of virtue that is not related in some sense to a picture of fighting, of struggle.

So those are the two fundamental sources of the anxiety about American religiosity.

TOJ: Do you think that those sources are in some ways seated in the—for lack of a better way of saying it—Protestant origin of American religion?

CM: Absolutely. I think that in some ways *Prophesies of Godlessness* builds on the critique of a relatively famous book by Sacvan Bercovitch, *The American Jeremiad*. Bercovitch's point is that a lot of the political discourse in the culture actually is rooted very much in the Protestant heritages, especially the Calvinist/Puritan heritage of a lot of Americans.[3] Josef Joffe, a German intellectual who edits the German weekly *Die Zeit*, makes the

2. Cavell, *Must We Mean What We Say?*
3. Bercovitch, *American Jeremiad*.

point that originally in Europe there were both Lutheran and Calvinist Protestants, but by in large, most of the Calvinists left. The Protestantism that is in Germany is a mostly Lutheran Protestantism; there are some Calvinists in Switzerland, of course, and in the Netherlands and Scotland, but historically, not that many. In fact, the majority of the Calvinists came to America. And it's funny when you talk to European Protestants—their experience of Protestantism is very different from the American experience of Protestantism, and it's because, effectively, the Calvinists left and came to the United States.

TOJ: Could you talk about how you understand this phenomenon within the context of atheism and the rise of secularism? Obviously this is something that isn't just happening now, so how do we understand this rise of secularism within America?

CM: One of the nice things about writing *Prophesies of Godlessness* was that it really educated me about some of the deep history of these tendencies. Two of the chapters in the book go back to people like Emerson and, of course, Jefferson, who is important to where I live here in Charlottesville, Virginia. These thinkers, while they were not what we would consider secularists of the sort that you would find in a humanist association, were in an important way engendering a more thorough deconstruction of ecclesial structures. In part, they thought this would accentuate and intensify other religiosities, but they also thought it would serve to secure the health of the future (in Emerson's mind) and the polity (in Jefferson's mind). And they proposed things that look a lot like what some of the secularists are proposing today.

More interestingly, at the end of the nineteenth century there was a much more vigorous and lively space for atheists in America. If you look at a work like Susan Jacoby's *Freethinkers*, she reports this long and interesting history of people who actually made a lot of money going on lecture circuits in the nineteenth century, like present-day Christopher Hitchenses, arguing religious points and everything.[4] It is interesting to think about a culture, then, that seemed to have a larger subunit that was susceptible to thinking about atheism as something one could consider as a live option or at least as something to be thinking about as an authentic

---

4. Jacoby, *Freethinkers: A History of American Secularism.*

arguing point. Now, what happens in the twentieth century that makes that goes away?

I think two things.

First, after World War I and the Scopes Trial, you get a more vocal fundamentalist wing of American Christianity, and this atheism is forced to retreat for a while. That's the story you get from George Marsden's work on fundamentalism[5] and Mark Noll's book *The Scandal of the Evangelical Mind.*[6] American religiosity became, in some ways, like the rest of the nation, much more consensual. Also, two ideologies emerged in the twentieth century that American religious historians don't think about too frequently, Nazism and Communism, and in a complicated way, both were profoundly anti-Christian. Thus, in a complicated way, atheism gets tarred indirectly with Nazism and much more profoundly with Communism. Christianity, or the civic religion, becomes a central bulwark in the fight against totalitarianism.

Now then, what was happening structurally? What was happening to the intellectual culture? If you believe people like Chris Smith and his colleagues in their book *The Secular Revolution*, who I happen to believe are right on this, the intellectual culture becomes much more secularized, as does the structure of the society,[7] because structures are created by the intelligentsia or the elite. Hence, the structures of the society become much more secularized, and the government becomes much more thoroughly managerial in its running.

After World War II, as other scholars have pointed out, the government takes over most of the social science obligations and social service obligations that the churches used to run. Also, the courts begin to move in a much more secularizing way, in part driven by people who seem to have read Paul Tillich and the Niebuhr brothers (Reinhold and H. Richard) in the course of their education. You get all these positions from the 1940s forward that seem to be investing themselves in a certain Tillichian definition of religion, it seems to me. So really, you get all this stuff that is all going on on the subsurface.

And again and again what you have happening are the structural conditions being put in place for a certain kind of much more efficiently

---

5. Marsden, *Fundamentalism and American Culture.*

6. Noll, *Scandal of the Evangelical Mind.*

7. C. Smith, *Secular Revolution.*

secular system, even though the broader and overarching culture turns out to be composed of very anxious, civic-religion Christians, of the "God and Country" variety.

Then from 1989 forward, with the collapse of the Soviet Union, the connection between atheism and anti-Americanism goes away. And then after 9/11, my god, suddenly it looks like atheism is not the main anti-Americanism at all.

This is why we are in a much different position than before. I don't think that American culture was necessarily tied up with a certain kind of religiosity, but the international conditions which really held it in place have declined precipitously in the last decade or so. So the example we gave of how American culture is still importantly religious is this wonderful essay we cited in our introduction called "Atheists as Others" by Penny Edgell, Joseph Gerteis, and Douglass Hartmann.[8] It is a sociological study of the different kinds of attitudes people have toward certain questions such as "Who would you like to have on your street?"; "Who would you like as president?"; and "Who would you like to teach your children?" And again and again, you can be gay, you can be of another race, you can be a man or woman, all of these things have become more acceptable than the one thing you cannot be: an atheist. Since the 1950s it seems that atheism has actually declined as a viable stance for a public figure to take. It's fascinating.

TOJ: Now, in speaking to that, let me ask a follow-up question in regard to the way atheism, or at least secularism, is related to a certain intellectual group of people. Do you think that in some ways the prophesies of godlessness that you named, and decline narratives in general, are juxtaposed to narratives of progress that emerged during that time? Is that primarily where they tend to live on, as a debate between intellectuals? Is it a dialectic within the intellectual culture or something else?

CM: Yeah, I think so. But I am not so sure I would call it a "dialectic." I would say that for some people they are complementary, whereas for other people, they are deeply opposed. But I think that one important strand of modern thought that in different ways emerges out of the French Enlightenment and the Scottish Enlightenment is this idea that a

8. Edgell, "Atheists as 'Other.'"

more worldly form of life is directly correlated with a kind of healthy and vigorous society that can grow, develop, and become more mature and disintegrated. And that progress is very clearly related to a certain kind of godlessness.

In the nineteenth century, it seems that an alternative German theory gets going which is more supple on this and seems to imply what some sociologists call "structuration." In other words, according to this theory, it's not so much that secularization will happen, but that a different kind of differentiation will happen and that religion can have a healthy place— this is a Jeffersonian line of thought, but it is found in Hegel, too—while still within a largely secular system. The problem there is that religion, as long as it plays nice with a certain vision of secularity, works well.

I think the best person in this tradition of thinking right now is a guy named José Casanova. He is not unaware of the blatantly antireligious dimensions to this, but he does not want to say that religion is going away or anything like that. And so his perspective is very interesting. Casanova points out that religion is not declining in the world—this is in the *Public Religions in the Modern World* book—but that what is happening is that religions are turning into denominations. There are no more state churches; there are only denominations.[9] I think that that is a very insightful point. Even if you do get a certain kind of secularization in the state, it is not a godlessness. It's just that religion becomes something that has to sit within a larger pedagogical schema. And my education, and I think your education too, suggests that religion doesn't like that. Religion wants to be its own fundamental framing picture; and I think for good reason it wants that. Talk about absolute faith! It can't necessarily be satisfied by playing nice in that way, nor should it.

TOJ: We are going to come back to that because I do want to ask you some questions about your book *A Theology of Public Life*—you've been a busy man lately! First, let's jump off in another direction. Could you frame for us some contemporary configurations of atheism? Are there different types of atheism? Is the atheism of Richard Dawkins and Christopher Hitchens similar or dissimilar to that of, say, Slavoj Žižek or some of the agonist political thinkers, like Carl Schmidt or Jacques Derrida, who you have interacted with in some of your writings?

9. Casanova, *Public Religions in the Modern World*.

CM: I think that they are very different kinds of people, but not so different that they are not centrally bound in the way that they critique religion. Although their critiques are very different, I find that it is what they affirm as part of their critiques that sets them apart. So agonists, one of my favorite agonists at least on a religious message is William Connolly, who wrote a really interesting book called *Why I Am Not a Secularist*. His argument, in that book anyway, is that secularism is in itself a kind of society that has the same kind of dogmatic unknowing that Nietzsche and others would have critiqued in certain kinds of religions. Now his critique of Christianity is not a critique that says I don't ever want to talk to it, his critique is rather that this is a really interesting debate we can have as long as we understand the debate in a certain way. I actually think that the way he understands the debate isn't bad.

Then there are people like Žižek, who, I confess, I think is really interesting and like the agonists in a certain way—although it's not so much agonism as it is a kind of psychosis or something. I really don't know what to call Žižek, apart from someone who I think could spend some time in the Betty Ford Clinic, but not because of any artificial substances; I think it is entirely generated by his own mind. He is clearly brilliant, but in the end, a book like *The Puppet and the Dwarf* seems in many ways to be a warmed-over kind of Marxism of a broad sort of atheistic liberation theology.

Then the people like Christopher Hitchens, or Sam Harris, or people like that—someone like Mark Lilla, though Lilla's not nearly as naive about it as, say, Hitchens, or Dawkins, or Harris—strike me as naively relying on certain kinds of slogans from the Enlightenment. I take their critiques of religion, and I think they are very valuable. I think that when you think about what they are trying to do, and people point this out, it seems like atheistic fundamentalism; it is going back to the fundamentals. The problem with that is that you are not confronting why the fundamentals were so dissatisfying in the first place. That is the problem with these thinkers.

There are very different ways of doing it. I think someone like Connolly or Žižek, when I have enough caffeine to understand him, or someone like Rom Coles—these figures are, I think, very interesting. Lilla I am not so sure about—in attempting to understand religion in the contemporary world, he turns to Rousseau, Hobbes, those sorts of thinkers— I mean, he seems committed to interpreting the world and its problems through his graduate school comprehensive exam reading lists, which is probably not the way I'd recommend trying to understand things. Coles and Connolly—they're the real deal.

TOJ: That provides a great segue to the next question, though I do want to come back and ask you about the difference between a theology of public life and a public theology, which I know you have answered in other places, but I would like for our readers to hear you answer the question. Before we do that, however, I know you've said that in wrestling with the agonists, particularly with people like Rom Coles, Carl Schmidt, and some of these other political philosophers we've noted, you've learned a lot from their ideas around conversation. Yet you also offer some criticisms of this type of thinking. Can you tell us, with respect to your Augustinian view of politics, what both can be learned from them and what are some of the problems with the agonist discussion?

CM: I think that agonists are fantastic, first of all, in terms of identifying more microscopically the tensions and ambivalences—this is where they are also related to Derrida—that lie at the heart not only of subjectivity but of any particular view that we might want to put forward. A sense that they have is that it is always better to allow the ambivalences and ambiguities of our views to emerge, to confront us, and to struggle with them than to let them be suppressed further from the surface. I think that is a very exciting and very promising thing compared to the ideas of many other political theorists, who want to offer a kind of picture of politics that is in some ways a kind of decision procedure, which doesn't allow a kind of residual sense of unfairness. It seems to be a wonderful and admirable project, in place of the Rawlsian-liberal project, where these theorists insist on the idea of fairness.

My point, which the agonists handle wisely, is that fairness is never total, and there are always going to be losers. In a way, the problem with liberals that agonists jump on, the problem with a certain kind of liberal, with a Rawlsian liberal—I don't want to say liberals in general because I think liberalism is a very heterogeneous thing—the problem with a certain kind of Rawlsian liberalism, which is not even Rawls's view, but a second-generation Rawlsianism—it is always the second generation that you have to worry about!—is that they simply don't have much in the way of resources to admit that there are losers, losers who could legitimately complain about the losses they suffer from any particular liberal consensus. The ideal that such thinkers—the Rawlsians, I mean—have is complete consensus, so they generate systems that seem really interested in denying dissent rather than acknowledging the legitimacy and existence of dissent.

So agonism is wonderful for that, for the political stuff, for the political debate, for understanding the complexities of human psychology and dialogue. Agonism's limitations, it seems to me, rest in its overly pessimistic ontology, which I say in my book actually naturalizes a certain kind of violence. In this way, I think someone like John Milbank has some important points to make about this. The agonists want to say that conflict is inevitable, and that seems to me to deny the phenomenology of conflict, which is the experience of the felt wrongness of conflict, the feeling you get when you're in it that it is wrong. When we experience conflict, it seems wrong. But they want, at least implicitly, to deny that. Because of this, there are also, I think, some problems with the psychology that agonism implies, a psychology that suggests to people—again, assuming that conflict is inevitable—that we need not really accommodate the possibility of a certain kind of integrity in human beings, the kind of integrity where that phenomenological experience of the felt wrongness of conflict tells us something important both about ourselves and about the nature of reality. They want to deny—or perhaps it's better to say that they seem structurally compelled to deny—that peoples' intuitions of this sort, profound intuitions—are either authentic or authentically tracking the truth. That's a major limitation.

TOJ: Right. That seems interesting in regard to the role that religion then plays in public life. And to the extent that Rawls, or someone like Richard Rorty, attempt to exclude all religion from public space and from public dialogue, it seems like the agonists in a certain way are opening public space to religious discourse and to beliefs and to serious concerns.

CM: That's probably why I am not a secularist. Absolutely!

TOJ: So in this sense, what way do you see these theorists changing the public space in American politics? Or are they? Maybe not?

CM: It might be, I think, that what we have is a series of confidences that are very interesting. We have the kind of crisis of intellectual confidence, of a certain kind of political liberalism, of the academic variety of the Rawlsian kind, and stuff like that. Sure, different things have happened to them—they have discovered that the world that they thought was coming about, both the secular world and the Democratic Party world, is not coming about, and that has caused such a difficulty for them. Essentially, some of the most powerful intellectual work in political philosophy these days is actually being done by Christians who are reacting to the Rawlsian project in different ways.

So it is a much more explosive, colorful religiosity that strikes me as permitting a certain kind of dialogue. But I also like to think that the great example of what went wrong with political liberalism, the great antidote that I love, is the fact that, as Allen Hertzke wrote in his book *Representing God in Washington* (a study about how different religious groups mobilize themselves to speak publicly in debates), the people who were most leaning to a liberal edict—that is, a restrained religious or faith edict— were actually the groups like Focus on the Family or the Family Values Commission. Even that language, "focus on the family," is not explicitly theological. People talk all the time about the Reverend James Dobson, but James Dobson isn't a reverend. He's a doctor; he's a medical doctor.

What's interesting is that people discovered that this idea of liberalism to restrain religious speech didn't work at all. So I think there is a way in which, intellectually, there is a new space for agonism. But then also, I think, one of the cultural advantages, in fact one of the advantages of the New Atheism, is that the New Atheists are around because people have realized, "Hey, wait a minute. It's OK for some people to be atheists." It is still quite shocking that in the public sphere the possibility of atheists has emerged again. And it's quite nice, because it is a really serious religiously pluriform public culture. We now have, especially after 9/11, vibrant Muslim voices in America.

TOJ: And that will lead us into the final question: Given that background and the kind of culture that we find ourselves in, can you give us the difference between a public theology and what you are trying to articulate as a theology of public life?

CM: Yes, chiefly, I want to step away from what I think the Hegelian/Jeffersonian project of attempting to articulate a common source of moral values for an entire society wanted to do. I don't know that we live in societies that have that kind of a common core of moral values. I am not saying we live in a totally fractured or divided society—I think there are lots of people, there are lots of ways in which we share many overlapping conclusions about various commitments. Some of them, I think, are very, very profound. However, I don't think they amount to a coherent, integrated picture of the fundamental values that everyone in our society does, or more menacingly, should endorse. What I see, instead, is a much more complicated non-Hegelian human community, where the debates about what is important or what is valuable are going on all the time, and many things are up for grabs.

I think that is OK. And in that situation what we need are not more attempts to try to articulate a kind of total uniform common ground, but rather, we need people attempting to explain "why" from a particular perspective or a specific vernacular. Like I say in *Prophesies of Godlessness*, what we need is a kind of vernacular; we need different ways of going out and engaging each other. A theology of public life is in several different ways one instance of this sort of thing.

Most obviously, it is a Christian topic because I think Christians are the central people talking about theology these days—to talk about Jewish "theology" or Muslim "theology" is at least to court mislocating, in terms of genre, the central intellectual energies in those traditions. And a theology of public life is an attempt to understand how public life, which is a broad term meaning politics but more than politics, has a role in the divine economy. That's what I try to do in the book. In the first part, I talk in general terms about what and how Augustine's work—which at its start tends to be escapist and interior, turning you inside and turning you away from public engagement, something diagnosed as solipsism—actually is a rich theological resource from which to propose a way of living as a form of engagement with the world.

Then, in part two, I lay this form of life out, trying to talk more fully and thoroughly about how the theological virtues can and should be exhibited in public life in different ways. That's what I am trying to do.

Now all that said, I want to be very clear on this. There are a lot of people who talk about doing public theology. But there are two problems with it. One is that I think the language of "public theology" can in itself be misleading. And the other problem is that the tradition of public theology seems to have a problematic history with which I don't want to encourage people to identify. But I have no problem with particular people talking about themselves as doing public theology or offering themselves as public theologians. It just depends on how you cash those terms out.

7

Three Questions on Modern Atheism:
An Interview with John Milbank

BEN SURIANO

The Other Journal (TOJ): It might seem appropriate to begin our interview by addressing the growing voice of this supposed New Atheism as represented by Richard Dawkins, Christopher Hitchens, Sam Harris, Daniel Dennett, Michel Onfray, et cetera, yet there seems to be nothing new here but a great display of amnesia concerning, among other things, their intellectual history. Moreover, what often passes for a religion/atheism discussion these days seems to be little more than a sensationalized intramural duel among real-life versions of Nietzsche's Last Man, as both atheists and religious interlocutors alike desperately try to assert moribund bourgeois ideals against one another.

However, despite the poverty and pettiness of its discourse, this particular cast of contemporary atheist and religious interlocutors has benefited from the media machine and its penchant for spectacles. Indeed, the popularization of New Atheism suggests that the late-capitalist culture industry is at work here, raising this spectacle to a reality, dominating the collective imagination, and transforming our understanding of what it means to be religious or scientific or atheistic, and perhaps this apparatus is what's really "new" here. Could you begin, then, by discussing the underlying logic of the culture industry, an industry to which both sides of the debate seem tied and which finds it necessary to produce, stage, and amplify this discussion/spectacle?

John Milbank (JM): I think that you have put this question really well and at a level of sophistication that is usually missing. It's as if the crude and dualistic presentation of issues so common in the media has now penetrated the book market and captured a part of what is supposedly serious discourse. For a long time now, the media has presented religion in terms of traditionalists—superstitious lunatic fundamentalists—versus liberal modernizers. This new shift seeks to imply that religion is fundamentally insanity, that its natural enemy is science, that liberal religious people are a bit confused, and that the only valid way to be a religious liberal is to be vaguely spiritual. I find it really hard to know what is going on here, so I can only offer some extremely tentative reflections.

It's important to note that the New Atheism movement began in the 1990s, well before 9/11, Dawkins, Dennett, and Paul Churchland had already got going.

Is this a purely Anglo-Saxon phenomenon? Not entirely. In French thought, there's been a gradual drift from post-structuralism (which, in retrospect, seems to be negative humanism after all) to new modes of speculative materialism. However, it's mainly in Anglo-Saxon countries that one gets the crude antireligion polemic. One might suggest that that's because the entire modernity-science-capitalism thing is at its most virulent here. Perhaps the French just give a softer, far more sophisticated version of this.

What needs to be focused on is the double impression given by the media: (1) religion is reviving and (2) clever people know that it is over. I find it fascinating that in Britain, which is of course far more modern than the United States, left versus right is increasingly seen as secular versus religious (though there are elements of this in the States). This is despite their recent history of conspicuously religious left-leaning political leaders.

One sees this phenomenon in the 2008 Parliament debate over an embryology bill. The press presented the debate as left versus right, science versus religion, et cetera and wrote naively as if science answered moral questions. But in reality, while the majority of left-wing members of Parliament supported experimentation on embryos, the fact that by no means all of them did so was, so to speak, hushed up. Increasingly, the media do not want complex stories, and they therefore make us live by this dualistic approach.

Yes, the spectacle of "science" is now regarded an absolute destiny. It is the human glory to undo itself through science. British police shows like *Waking the Dead* now screen very long takes of the dissection of human bodies by glamorous women. The message is that science is beautiful and glossy, that finding scientific truth is the one moral impulse, and that human life is otherwise a tragic mess.

Dawkins and his cohorts want the supposed incompatibility of science with religious belief to be *taught* as an official part of a state agenda. This is tantamount to a revival of Soviet-style official atheism. It would mean that the obvious "debatability" of this view would be denied and free speech would therefore be denied to one side of the debate. Religious people, as declaredly "anti-science," would inevitably become second-class citizens. But I'm not arguing on "liberal" grounds here for the equality of all and every opinion, I'm rather suggesting that some issues have to be publicly regarded as "debatable" even though one stands on one side or another. Hence, I would argue that it is "radically irrational" to suppose that people who think religion and science are compatible are "obviously stupid." But I would also argue the reverse. People who think religion and science are incompatible are in my view mistaken and not subtle thinkers, but I can see how they have made this mistake for apparently plausible-sounding reasons. There is no need to marginalize them as lunatics—though the case for doing so would be far rationally stronger than the case for marginalizing religious people.

What's this new scientistic fanaticism all about? Well, I suppose it is fundamentally about the collapse of all secular ideologies in the late twentieth century. One is left with the truth of science as the only reality of the modern. If science is simply the freedom to know, it can become Faustian. And apart from this freedom, there is only the right to choose one's own lifestyle. The crucial thing here that the Left has missed is that sexual freedoms have increased exponentially while all other freedoms have declined.

Today in Great Britain, you scarcely have the right to demonstrate, and a higher proportion of Great Britain's population is in prison than the proportion of China's population that is in prison. The boy at the shop counter with no customers is not allowed to read a book to improve himself, but who cares what he gets up to with sex and drink after the shop closes? Of course, there's also a doublethink about sex—it's all OK and yet male sexuality is nearly always exploitative, et cetera—but in general, it would seem that, as Theodor Adorno and Max Horkheimer and Herbert

Marcuse predicted, sexualization is intended to keep us all quiet: neurotic, hysterical, frustrated, and unhappy but still "looking." Knowing that they can watch a porn film when they get home from work, workers may overlook the fact that they have lost the lunch hour when they could have caught up with public affairs over a sandwich in the local library.

Thus, with sex divided from procreation, science and sexual freedom come together in a tacit Malthusian program of biopolitical manipulation. The state aspires both scientifically to control reproduction and to keep its citizens drugged with dreams of sex and the need to compete in the sexual agon. Michel Houellebecq is completely right about this, and the Left has to rethink its 60s-derived libertarianism if it wishes to continue to oppose capitalism.

Instead, by supporting the total disjuncture of sex and procreation, the Left is really supporting a new mode of fascism. "Women" are lined up with science and choice in order to produce a new kind of ideal human subjectivity—male and autonomous and yet pliant in a "female" manner. The re-envisaged autonomous female body is the final site of the coming together of scientific objectivity and absolute freedom of choice. Perhaps one could even speak here of a new racism of the human race as such—it's to be made the object of an endless "objective" improvement and the expression of a will to freedom/will to power. Of course, this also means that the specific phenomenology of the female body is destroyed. It's denied that this body is inherently linked both to the male body (as also vice versa) and to another body that is itself and yet becomes not itself—the baby. Having denied the link of babies to men and also to women, save as objects of their ("male") choice, babies thereby become pure consumer objects, and all human relationality and personhood is abandoned.

After the collapse of secular ideologies, then, one is left with "just science." But also, of course, "the return of religion," since these now represent the only alternative ideologies—virulent in the case of Islam where religion is still overwhelmingly practiced.

Post-9/11 has allowed the media to present the religion-versus-science story in ever cruder terms. Of course, it's highly significant that Hitchens also supported the Bush foreign policy. This is because, at bottom, neoliberalism and scientism line up with each other. But Hitchens never really explains how his imperialism of reason relates to the messianic aspect of American imperialism. He and others don't explore the point at which fundamentalism and scientism can be in a hidden alliance in that the very emptiness of a formalist approach to economics and politics can allow an extreme religiosity to supply the concrete content. Racist and nationalist fascism can no longer do this very readily because races are mixed up and national identities are confused—so one is getting regionalism as much as nationalism. Religions, by contrast, supply diffused globalized identities so that religious extremism fits well with an era of globalization. Yet so also does naturalism, the idea that all we have in common is one material planet and our physical nature.

Hence, the age of religious and philosophical "agnosticism" is over—as Quentin Meillassoux says. Now we have two rival dogmatisms about the infinite: materialism and fundamentalism.

Instead of these dire alternatives, we need more apophatic (though not agnostic) approaches to the infinite; we need to recognize that, as Charles Taylor says, many people embrace a complex mix of belief and unbelief, and as Pope Benedict XVI advocates, we need more subtle mixes of faith and reason.[1]

But the only way our media would recognize this complexity is if we were not dominated by capitalism in the mode of the spectacle.

TOJ: In considering the historical development of modern atheism's cultural logic, what would you consider as its defining cultural form, if there is such a thing? That is, what has been continuously present throughout its modern history? Moreover, what key shifts in the way that power was constructed, distributed, and organized, especially through changing socioeconomic formations, might have provided the necessary material conditions for its emergence and particular shape?

JM: I think that we've scarcely begun to pose, much less explore, this all-important question. How is it that atheism arose so recently—at the end of eighteenth century—and yet so quickly established itself? Clearly, it began as an elite phenomenon, so it is from the start and up to now socially connected to the idea of a new, rival elite opposed to the old aristocracy. This means that it has to be considered a bourgeois phenomenon or else one of decadent aristocracy—which is another modern socializing mode.

1. For this and all future references to Taylor, see *A Secular Age*. Also, see Pope Benedict XVI's Regensburg address, "Faith, Reason, and the University."

I think that Charles Taylor, in *A Secular Age*, provides important clues by saying that the atheist self is the "buffered self"—no external spiritual forces can get to it—and also that it is a self that is entirely in charge of its own morality and self-disciplining. Thus, as he argues, if Latin Christianity, because of its over-disciplinary mode and its "festive" deficit, ushered in this sort of self, atheism finally dispenses with the religious bit altogether. This atheist self is definitely the self that is totally autonomous, and so it likes to reduce everything to predictable calculation. Spiritual security and worldly freedom and comfort are preferred over the aristocratic heroism of a quest for meaning. In Great Britain, even up to, say, Prime Minister Thatcher or even Blair, the establishment was still somewhat religious. But Blair, ironically, ushered in a new political class that saw politics like a business that is to be exploited, and this political class is essentially an atheist class. Maybe the explicit personal religiosity of the New Labour party in some way worked ideologically to mask this.

To my mind, then, modernity is liberalism, liberalism is capitalism—"political economy"—and capitalism is atheism and nihilism. Not to see this, or rather not fully to see this, is the critical deficit of Marxism. Again, Taylor is right: all critical resistance to modernity is "romantic" in character. It (1) allows that more freedom and material happiness is a partial good, (2) yearns for elements of lost organic values, and (3) realizes that the anti-body, anti-festivity, anti-sex, hell-linked, disciplinary, over-organized character of Latin Christendom is ironically responsible for the Enlightenment mentality.

I'm starting to think that this triple romanticism is more fundamental than any left/right characterization, which after all, is a kind of accidental result of the French Revolution. Both Left and Right, as André de Muralt argues in *L'unite de la philosophie politique*, are nominalist: both favor a strong, single center of money or power or both (Right), or the rights of the many singly or when totted up (Left). Both positions are also, in the end, atheist.

It is also important now to reread carefully Karl Polanyi's *The Great Transformation*, arguably the most important work of political economy written in the last century. Although it is a socialist work, which indeed goes rigorously beyond Marx's ontology and history of capitalism from a "religious," guild-socialist perspective, it is also suspicious of most socialisms—state socialism, certainly, but also many associative socialisms, which he notably tracks back to late seventeenth-century Quaker thought. Polanyi sees these as all too akin to capitalist attempts to make indigency and impoverishment a paradoxical source of wealth. Instead, he favors both wide distribution of assets (like G. K. Chesterton and Hilaire Belloc) and a guild-restriction of market entry, which by limiting market competition actually *protects* market competition from monopoly. This allows "reciprocity" to rule—the primacy of mutual satisfaction of needs. This, he argues, is the human norm against Adam Smith. And against Friedrich Hayek, Polanyi is saying that reciprocity is the norm of *markets*. German ordoliberalism or "social market" theory has often said the same thing. Maurice Glasman, in *Afflicted Powers*,[2] has shown how the British Left has misunderstood this current and how close it is to both Polanyi and to Catholic social teaching. One can also note in passing that Polanyi praises Archbishop William Laud and condemns the Cromwellian commonwealth with respect to their treatment of the poor! It is a Catholic not a Protestant socialism that he points us toward.

We need, indeed, a new kind of romantic politics that is specifically religious, and often Christian, in thinking that one can only get distributive equality on the basis of agreed upon values and an elite transmission and guarding of those values. A more Carlylean and Ruskinian politics then—basically left, yet with elements that are not really right so much as premodern and traditionalist. Strictly speaking, the premodern predates Right versus Left. In Great Britain, Phillip Blond is developing a crucially important new mode of Red Toryism, which might in my view be seen as a kind of traditionalist socialism. This is already having a profoundly transformative effect upon British politics and, in effect, marks the political translation of the paradox of Radical Orthodoxy and the beginning of its entry upon the political stage. Red Toryism is also rapidly acquiring a global influence. Others have been speaking of a "blue socialism" (e.g., myself) or of "blue labour" (e.g., Maurice Glasman, a Polanyist Jewish socialist, and Jon Cruddas, a prominent Labour member of Parliament). However, I would argue that the paradox amounts to the same thing whatever way one puts it. Blond draws upon genuine traditions of Tory radicalism (Richard Oastler, etc.) but in fact Red Toryism goes well beyond that. It stakes out a new radical communitarian ground against the liberalism of both Right and Left.

2. See Retort, *Afflicted Powers*.

The hard thing now for critical thinkers to do is to think outside leftism. They have to see that if neoliberalism and neoconservatism have totally triumphed, this is because the Left in its traditional mode is incapable of carrying out an adequate critique of capitalism. In the end, this is because it's atheistic—one needs to be religious to recognize objective values and meanings as not just epiphenomenal. Again, Polanyi clearly saw that capitalist "primary accumulation" is always also an act of desacralization. Today in Great Britain, the Left is more or less now defining itself as scientistic, which as I mentioned earlier, actually permits an underwriting of a new mode of fascism and racism.

Left Christians now must stress the Christian bit much more if they are truly going to be able to make a critical intervention.

Atheism is bourgeois oppression; atheism is the opium of the people—it claims to discover an ontology that precludes all hope. In the face of this, we need now to celebrate the faithful legacy of peasants; learned, honorable, and genuinely paternalist aristocrats; Christian warrior-kings like Alfred the Great and Charles Martel; yeomen farmers and self-sacrificial scholars—Charles Péguy, William Cobbett, and Hilaire Belloc are the men for the hour.

TOJ: How might we understand the key intellectual shifts that both made possible and legitimated the changes in the organization of power which contributed to the rise of modern atheism? Moreover, in light of the common readings of atheism as essentially negative—as a sober desacralizing, disenchanting, and demythologizing movement—how should we understand the intellectual shifts of modern atheism in relation to Christian theology? Did atheism's intellectual development come by way of a thorough rejection of theology, as common readings claim, or more primarily as the construction of an alternative theology?

JM: Again, this is to ask absolutely the right question. Many authors, like Michael Buckley, have now shown that atheism was not "subtractive."[3] In the face of a decadent late-Baroque theology, it had positively to invent a self-sufficient naturalism, or else new modes of theism were invented. Often, indeed, atheism has operated as a religion—of nature, of man, of race, of class destiny—and now it's becoming the religion of science—

3. See Buckley, *At the Origins of Modern Atheism.*

democracy is supposed to produce an obedient seconding of the verdicts of science, which are seen as answering all problems, even ethical ones.

Taylor has now extended the anti-subtraction theory into the social realm. The very idea of social and political order without religion is bizarre by all traditional lights. The invention of secular order is an extraordinary achievement, if not highly questionable, because instead of faith, it requires rational foundations that one really can't have. Thus, practical atheism is more dogmatic than religion.

I'd add to Taylor a bigger stress on the dubiousness of liberalism, which is mainly political economy. As Pierre Manent argues in *An Intellectual History of Liberalism*, liberalism "empties the soul"—it delivers negative freedom at the price of a loss of character.

We're now at a crossroads. Politics has become a shadow play. In reality, economic and cultural liberalism go together and increase together. The Left has won the cultural war, and the Right has won the economic war. But of course, they are really both on the same side.

The point is to resist this. And that means, of course, to rethink Christendom, but in more festive, pro-body terms, yet more interpersonal, less fearing terms, and terms that celebrate much more excellence and virtue in every realm, including those of craft, farming, and trade, and to rethink Christendom with greater will to the democratization of excellence.

The "other religions" thing in the end won't matter. The world as a whole is rapidly Christianizing, and even in Islamic countries like Bangladesh, Muslims are finding their own specific and valuably Islamic way to Christ in notably increasing numbers. As Paul Claudel realized in *Le Soulier de Satin,* the meaning of globalization is a shift to the primacy of the sea, *la mer tout entière,* and so figurally of baptism and personal relationship, however terrestrially sundered. The evil disasters of colonialism can only be redeemed when they are seen as perverse and yet providential ways to the further proclamation of Christian universalism.

But the challenge now is to have a good and true and not a perverted capitalist version of a global Christendom.

8

Atheism for Lent

Merold Westphal

Atheism is hot right now. Books by Richard Dawkins, Sam Harris, Christopher Hitchens, and others have gotten a good deal of attention.[1] But we should not misinterpret their significance. They are, I suspect, preaching to the choir.

Not many people become Christians by reading, say, the apologetic writings of C. S. Lewis. The main consumers of apologetic writings are believers and readers with a fairly strong inclination in that direction. It is partly a matter of faith (actual or incipient) seeking understanding and probably, more importantly, faith seeking reassurance. Believers understand that we walk by faith and not by sight, but they don't wish to think of that faith as blind, arbitrary, or irrational. Apologetic writings articulate the internal rationale in terms of which belief(s) makes sense.

Very likely it is the same with atheistic apologetics. Not many atheists (or self-described agnostics who act as if they were atheists) got to where they are because they became disenchanted with proofs for the existence of God, just as very few believers came to belief by finding these proofs convincing. Psychological, social, and moral factors play a large role in both directions. I suspect that atheistic apologetics play a similar role to theistic or explicitly Christian apologetics. Unbelievers, in

1. See for instance Harris, *Letter to a Christian Nation*; Hitchens, *God Is Not Great*; Dennett, *Breaking the Spell*; Dawkins, *God Delusion*.

The potentially surprising suggestion of my essay title, "Atheism for Lent," is taken from a chapter title in my book *Suspicion and Faith*. Some churches, I am told, have developed Lenten study groups in keeping with this suggestion. The reader is referred to this volume for more detailed development of the atheisms of Marx, Nietzsche, and Freud, and of their possible appropriation by believers.

this case, who got where they are by a very complicated and not entirely intellectual process, are happy to be assured that they are being rational in their unbelief.

It is important, however, to distinguish between two kinds of atheism. One kind, which we may call evidential atheism, focuses on such questions as whether it is possible to prove the existence of God or to prove the non-existence of God, especially in relation to the obvious existence, extent, and intensity of evil in the world. Or in a less ambitious manner, these evidential atheists ask whether it is rational to believe or to not believe. Rationality is a lower hurdle, because it can be rational to believe something that turns out to be false. Thus, children who believe what their parents tell them are neither acting irrationally nor violating any cognitive duties, even when their parents may be mistaken on this or that point. Similarly, although it turned out that Saddam Hussein wasn't stockpiling weapons of mass destruction before the United States' 2003 invasion, it may still have been rational for Colin Powell to believe that Hussein had such weapons. In contrast, if the charges against Dick Cheney of "cherry-picking" intelligence are true, it may have been irrational for him to have the same belief as Powell. Unlike truth, rationality is person relative. One and the same belief may be rationally held by one person but only irrationally by another.

So evidential atheism revolves around the questions: Can we know (with reasonable certainty) that God does or does not exist? And would it be rational or irrational to believe that God exists?

Another kind of atheism, the atheism of suspicion, employs the *hermeneutics of suspicion*. Theologians are familiar with the term hermeneutics, which signifies reflection on interpretation, in connection with questions about how to interpret the Bible. However, in the present context, the term has a slightly different meaning. First, it is not a normative, how-to enterprise, but a descriptive theory (or range of theories) making the claim that our understanding is interpretative in nature. Rather than pure intuitions in which our mind passively mirrors the world or the meaning of the text, understanding is an active construal of its meaning in a context where other construals are always possible. Second, the suggestion is that it is not just in theology or law that interpretation matters but rather, that often or even always our understanding is interpretive in nature, not only in academic disciplines but also in everyday life.

But the key term here is suspicion. Our interpretations are guided by suspicion when we construe a belief or practice as involving self-deception. The suspicion is that while we understand our beliefs and practices in terms that are honorable or at least innocent, what is really going on underneath is darker and more shameful by our own standards. Hence, we hide it from ourselves. We speak of justice in relation to our belief in and practice of capital punishment, but Nietzsche suspects that what is really at work is revenge. Similarly, in Freudian language, our dream (in its manifest content) of an uncle may seem innocent but its true meaning (its latent content) is suggestive of our jealous rivalry with a colleague.

Or we can take a lighter example from Gilbert and Sullivan's *Pirates of Penzance.*[2] When Frederick, an apprentice pirate, is doing a bit of R & R on the Cornish beach and comes across a bevy of nubile maidens (who turn out to be the daughters of the Modern Major General), he asks if there is not one of them who in the name of duty would marry him and rescue him from his involuntary piracy. Being properly Victorian young ladies, they all most emphatically say no—all except the beautiful Mabel. Scolding her sisters for their lack of pity or compassion, she says she is willing. And without any special training, these women show themselves to be masters of the hermeneutics of suspicion. They sing:

> The question is, had he not been
> A thing of beauty,
> Would she be swayed by quite as keen
> A sense of duty?

If the casting director has been lucky, Frederick and Mabel don't just have beautiful voices. He is a hunk, and she is a babe. He has been reading his Kant (on a pirate ship?), and he states his case in the language of duty. She has been reading her Aristotle (as a Victorian maiden?), and she states her case in the language of virtue (pity, compassion). But beneath this lofty disguise with which the two young lovers deceive themselves, the sisters see all too easily that what is really driving the scene is ordinary, everyday sex appeal.

The late French philosopher Paul Ricoeur has called Marx, Nietzsche, and Freud the "masters of suspicion."[3] These three, of course, are perhaps

2. Gilbert and Sullivan, *The Pirates of Penzance.*
3. Ricoeur, *Freud and Philosophy,* 32.

the most widely influential atheists of the nineteenth and twentieth centuries. But they are not evidential atheists. They do not try to disprove the existence of God or to show theistic belief to be irrational with reference to the lack of evidence for or the weight of evidence against such belief. To these thinkers, atheism is best seen as axiomatic; the question is not whether there is a God of the sort that the Abrahamic monotheisms affirm but rather, because "we know" that there is not such a God, how can we explain why such belief is so widespread and so powerful? As masters of suspicion, they suspect that while theistic believers describe their religion in intellectually and morally honorific terms, the deepest motives and operative functions of belief are less lofty and for that reason are kept out of sight (of the believer if not of the suspicious unbeliever).

We can thus define the hermeneutics of suspicion at work in these atheisms, as I have written elsewhere, as "the deliberate attempt to expose the self-deceptions involved in hiding our actual operative motives from ourselves, individually or collectively, in order not to notice how and how much our behavior and our beliefs are shaped by values we profess to disown."[4]

Before turning to the three atheisms before us, there are several things we might notice about the hermeneutics of suspicion as a general practice.

Beliefs that are exposed by suspicion to be less than lofty may nevertheless be true. Thus, for example, I may believe a piece of nasty gossip, for which I have no supporting evidence, because of my hatred or jealousy toward the person involved. My believing is shameful, but the belief may still be true. We would be committing the "genetic fallacy" to assume that a badly held belief is necessarily false. Quite possibly Dan Rather was too eager to believe that George W. Bush had shirked his duty in the National Guard. The suspicion that he was for this reason insufficiently critical of his source cost him his job. But his belief may well be true nevertheless.

In this area, it is often quite easy to play that *tu quoque* game. That's Latin for "it takes one to know one." Thus, in response to Freud's claim that theistic belief is infantile, it is easy enough to reply that his atheism is an adolescent rebellion against any parental authority. But we should notice (1) that this does not settle the question of truth, (2) that both

4. Westphal, *Suspicion and Faith*, 13.

charges might be right, and (3) that there may be, as I will suggest, a more appropriate response for the believer.

Truth is no defense against the charges leveled by suspicion. It may well be, for example, that the convicted defendant deserves to be sentenced to a long prison term or even to death. But the speeches made to this effect by the family of the victim at a sentencing hearing may be expressions of little more than hatred and revenge. Similarly, even if theistic belief is true, the believings may be vulnerable to and discredited by the critiques of suspicion. Frederick would have missed the point of the sister's gibe if he tried to argue that they really had a duty to help him, just as it would be beside the point for Mabel to insist that the sisters really were lacking in compassion.

Suspicion is most easily practiced by "us" against "them," whoever "we" and "they" may be. Thus, atheists against believers and vice versa, or Democrats against Republicans and vice versa. But this is not necessary, and so when I defined the hermeneutics of suspicion, I deliberately used "our" instead of "their" in order to suggest that, while we may get good at suspicion by practicing it on "them," its proper function may be to practice it upon ourselves in a kind of Lenten self-examination, worrying about the log in our own eyes before going after the speck in theirs (Matt 7:1–5).

What if the biblical prophets, apostles, and Jesus himself were the originators of suspicion against the piety of the covenant people of God? What if Marx, Nietzsche, and Freud are plagiarists, who should have footnoted their biblical sources? What if today's believers should explore the religious uses of these modern atheisms before trying to refute them? What if their critiques are all too true all too much of the time? If "all our righteous deeds are like a filthy cloth" (Isa 64:6) and "The heart is devious above all else" (Jer 17:9), then believers, too, might be among those "who by their wickedness suppress the truth" (Rom 1:18), creating God in our image and in accord with our own desires.

That is just what Freud says, noting, as if to protect himself from my plagiarism charge, that his psychological analysis agrees with religion (in substance if not in language) in the claim that we are all miserable sinners. Believers are self-deceived about what is really going on, both in their beliefs and their practices. Freud says that religious beliefs are like dreams and religious practices like the rituals of obsessional neuroses (for example, Lady Macbeth's hand washing compulsion). The latter comparison is too complex to be treated here, so we will direct ourselves to the cognitive dimension of religion, which in any case is the scene for the question of theism versus atheism.

To call religious beliefs analogs of dreams is to say that they are disguised wish fulfillments. For Freud, adult dreams, at least the ones he finds of interest, are representations of the satisfaction of forbidden desires, especially sexual or aggressive (hateful) desires. But because these desires are forbidden, their naked (no pun intended) representation would be too costly for us in terms of the guilt such representations would produce. So in dreaming, we disguise the fulfillment so as to have the best of both worlds. The manifest content is an innocent, if puzzling representation, whereas the latent content provides the forbidden emotional satisfaction while remaining hidden from view.

To Freud, this is also how religious beliefs work. What we would like is a God at our disposal, a powerful father figure who will take care of us, protect us from the indifference of nature's forces, including both death and the rigid demands of society and culture. In addition to being a Providential Power, we would like to have a Moral Lawgiver and Judge who would be sure to give our enemies what they've got coming. But in relation to ourselves, we'd like to see the moral dimension relaxed, in such a way that the Heavenly Father is more like a doting grandfather. It is as if we wanted to be able to pray:

> Our Father, who art in heaven,
> hallowed be my name.
> My kingdom come,
> my will be done
> on earth as yours is in heaven.[5]

Of course, the believer is too pious to pray in such a blatant manner, so the more familiar words are used. But Freud suspects that we deceive ourselves and that the deepest motivation and the operative function of the prayer is more truthfully expressed in this version that when undisguised sounds blasphemous.

The God we really mean, as distinct from the God we persuade ourselves that we mean, is indeed created in our own image. But not *ex*

5. The example is mine, not Freud's.

nihilo (out of nothing), not from whole cloth. All that is required is a little (or a lot of) editing. It's a little like political spin—one doesn't abandon factuality altogether; one only redescribes it in favor of oneself or one's party, distorting the truth in the process. Similarly, in the theological case, one takes a reality that the unbeliever wouldn't question, say the Highest Power, which for the atheist might well be nature or matter, and describes it as our Loving Heavenly Father. Or again, one's point of departure might be the biblical God whom one (or a whole tradition or community) edits to be more congenial and less demanding. Thus, Bonhoeffer can speak of "cheap grace" and Kierkegaard can speak of "paganism in Christendom," *nota bene*. These last two instances show that atheism does not have a monopoly on the hermeneutics of suspicion. It is also (and I would argue, originally) found in the prophetic strands of biblical religion and in theologies that haven't edited them down to the place where their critical voice is effectively silenced.

Whereas for Freud, theistic belief is our weakness before the forces of nature and society seeking consolation, for Marx theistic belief is social power, economic and political, seeking legitimation. In his vocabulary, it is *ideology*. He uses this term in a narrower and more specific sense than we normally do. For us ideology signifies a political philosophy, a body of ideas that articulates a fairly determinate political, social, and economic ethos. For Marx, however, it signifies such ideas in their role as providing legitimation for the dominant social order. Thus, as he and Engels put it in the *Communist Manifesto*, "The ruling ideas of each age have ever been the ideas of its ruling class."[6]

Marx sees society as composed of three strata. The most fundamental of these three being the economic system, the means of production, and the relations of production. But ever since primitive communism (when the plains Indians get buffalo, everyone eats, and when they don't, nobody eats), the slaves of antiquity, the serfs of feudalism, and the wage laborers of modern capitalism have been exploited by those who owned the means of production (primarily land until the industrial revolution).

Such systems require enforcement, and Marx suggests that political systems play that role. But force by itself is never enough. It needs to be supplemented by consent, or at least by compliance. So moral, legal, metaphysical, and religious ideologies come onto the scene to provide

6. Marx and Engels, *Manifesto of the Communist Party*, section 2.

theoretical justification of the political-economic system. In this mix of ideas, Marx highlights the role of religious ideas because nothing provides a stronger legitimation of a social order than when people believe it to be the will of God. So while religion sees itself in terms of lofty metaphysical truths and moral ideals, Marx is suspicious that its primary function is to put the divine stamp of approval on the current form of exploitation. (This is closely related to the claim that all wars are, at base, "holy" wars, justified by some theistic or secular religion such as communism or democracy.)

For this reason, Marx is not surprised to find that the working class in England is not conspicuously pious—Sundays are their only respite from an oppressive workweek—whereas the American slaves are frequently described as pious. He thus notes that Christianity as an ideology does its legitimizing work partly by offering justification to the beneficiaries of exploitation and partly by offering consolation to its victims: there is a better world awaiting just over Jordan in Beulah Land, and in heaven all "God's chillun' got shoes."[7] In slave religion, hope weakens the impetus toward rebellion. However, the focus of ideology critique in Marx is the way religion assuages the consciences of those who live off the labor of others so that they can, for example, go to church in the morning and come home to whip their slaves in the afternoon.

While Marxian theory calls our attention to the important role religion has played in the legitimation of such social systems as slavery, apartheid, and segregation, it tends to be blind to the role of religion in the anti-slavery movement, the anti-apartheid movement, and the civil rights movement. Religion, it would appear, is Janus-faced. It can be used to do the devil's work, and it can function as a prophetic critique of social sin. In general, the masters of suspicion identify a spot at which theistic belief is undeniably vulnerable and talk as if that were the whole story about Christianity. So it is tempting for believers to call attention to this one-sidedness, and, in the case of Marx, to call attention to the atrocities accomplished in Marx's name. But if such a "defense" is left at that, it is doubly defective. On the one hand, it is a refusal to take Jesus seriously about the priority of the log in "our" own eyes over the speck in "theirs."

---

7. This phrase is quoted from the Negro Spiritual "All God's Chillun Got Wings." For a comprehensive and classic study of Christianity's relationship to North American slavery, see Raboteau, *Slave Religion*.

On the other hand, it is a refusal to recognize that even if the Marxian critique of Christianity is one-sided, the side to which he calls our attention has been all too true all too much of the time. It is a reality and not a fiction.

The use of the past tense here points to a last, desperate attempt to miss the point. We can congratulate ourselves on having slavery, apartheid, and the Jim Crow South behind us. We have sided, at least after the fact, with those who in the name of faith opposed these evils. But all too easily, we become like the Sunday school teacher who taught a lesson on the Pharisee and tax collector who went up to the temple to pray, the former in self-righteous complacency, the latter in repentant humility (Luke 18:9–14), and concluded by saying, "Now, children, let us bow our heads, fold our hands, close our eyes, and thank God that we are not like that Pharisee."

To read Marxian atheism for Lent is not to find some way to dismiss or discredit this version of suspicion. It is, rather, to let ourselves, individually and collectively, be cross-examined so as to uncover the ways in which we are self-deceived about the social function of our piety. It is well to remember that the German Christians lent their support to the Nazi regime by their own anti-Semitism, whether it was vocally overt or silently complicit. (Lord, I thank Thee that I am not like those Germans.) Piety that is silent in the face of social injustice is as vulnerable to Marxian critique as overt support for oppression of various kinds. For silence, too, is the consent that lends legitimacy.

If for Marx, religion, especially Christianity, primarily functions as ideological legitimation of social power,[8] for Nietzsche it primarily functions as the lower class's verbal revenge for their social weakness. The strong (the rich and powerful) think of themselves as good, but in a sociological rather than a moral sense. They are noble rather than base, the elite rather than the *hoi polloi*, the upper crust rather than the crumbs or the disposable leftovers of the social order. They are the masters over and against the slaves. Nietzsche uses slavery terms in an expanded sense; beyond the institution of slavery as such, he uses them to signify the

---

8. A reminder: Rather than focusing on the question of truth, the hermeneutics of suspicion looks for hidden motivations that are often best revealed in actual functions or uses. For our three atheistic masters of suspicion, the question of truth is already settled and doesn't need to be argued, or at best, only very briefly.

fundamental distinction between the dominant and the dominated in any social order.

Nietzsche insists that it is the "slave revolt in morality"[9] that makes "good" the opposite of "evil," especially in the context of biblical religion. As we might by now suspect, it is not that God in heaven gives a law that commands some things as goodness and forbids others as evil. The story rather goes like this: The slaves have no power, physical or social, with which to punish their oppressors, thereby wreaking their revenge and satisfying their resentment. So they use the only weapon available to them: language. They call their masters "evil." This is because the masters fail to accept the constraints placed upon their otherwise unfettered power by the "good" as required by the new ethic of altruism and asceticism. With the help of their intellectuals, whom Nietzsche identifies as the priestly caste,[10] the slaves give birth to the dominant morality of the West and the religions, Judaism and Christianity, that are its primary bearers. God functions as the primary source and enforcer of the new values, "good" and "evil."

These religions speak much of neighbor love and social justice, but Nietzsche believes that what is really at work on the dark underside of these pieties is a spirit of resentment and revenge. Thus, where the manifest content is justice, he suspects that the latent content is revenge; and where the manifest content is pity or compassion, he suspects that the latent motive is to establish one's own superiority, not only materially but especially morally. No doubt Nietzsche assumes too quickly that this is the whole story about the moralities and monotheisms of Judaism and Christianity; and no doubt his theory would not have had the survival power it has shown if there had not been more than a grain of truth in it. Just as the prophet Nathan boldly told David, "Thou art the man," so Nietzsche accuses theists of self-righteous self-deception, trying to hide from others and successfully hiding from ourselves the ways in which our pieties serve our individual and collective wills to power. Nietzsche would not be surprised, for example, to find Christians on both sides of the abortion debate all too eager to dub their opponents evil, not only

9. Especially as developed in Nietzsche, *On the Genealogy of Morality*.

10. Here, again, the term has an extensive reference. It surely applies to the clergy, but beyond that, it applies to all those who, in Marxian language, might be called the ideologues of the slaves, all those who base morality and legality as well as religion on the distinction between good and evil.

because of their beliefs and practices relating to the substantive issue, but also, in a second level of Nietzschean name-calling, precisely for their eagerness to call "us" on the other side of the issue evil.

The critiques of religion by these three masters of suspicion have an irony to them. They accuse Christians and others of worshiping idols, gods created by their own thoughts in the service of their own not very pious desires. In discussing this trio with a group of students at a Christian college, I once said that I thought I had probably never prayed to a God who wasn't an idol. Their immediate reaction made it clear that they were as horrified as they were puzzled. So I explained. I thought that the God who hears my prayers is not an idol but the maker of heaven and earth. However, God as represented by me and to me in my prayers is always to a greater or lesser degree edited, both by me and by the traditions that have shaped me. It is not just my finitude that makes my ideas inadequate to the reality of God (though I think this is certainly true); it is also the sinful desires by which I and the traditions by which I have been formed have suppressed the truth by revising God (Rom 1:18). The students got the point and became very sober.

Luther would have understood more quickly. He writes, "Through sin we are completely turned away from God, so that we do not think correctly about God but think of Him simply as we do of an idol."[11]

We can speak here of the Third Commandment idolatry:[12] "You shall not make wrongful use of the name of the LORD your God" (Exod 20:7). Taking the Lord's name in vain is not just a matter of swearing: we violate this commandment whenever we put our theistic, even our specifically Christian, beliefs and practices in the service of our own interests insofar as they have not been fully brought into conformity with God's will. Just to that degree, we make God into a fictitious fulfiller of our wishes (Freud), whether this be to underwrite our own privilege (Marx) or to undermine the good name of those we dislike (Nietzsche).

So the atheisms of these three masters of suspicion may well be helpful aids in Lenten self-examination leading to repentance. There are, however, three dangers to be alerted to in using atheism for Lent. First, if we fall in love with practicing suspicion on "them," leaving its practice upon ourselves and our communities for tomorrow and tomorrow and

---

11. Luther, *Luther's Works*, 12:309.

12. For Catholics and Lutherans it would be Second Commandment idolatry.

tomorrow, we lapse into the phariseeism that has never been the monopoly of those whom Jesus opposed in his earthly ministry. Second, just to the degree that we begin to see the universality of sin as an epistemic category, a distorter of religious as well as irreligious beliefs, we can become cynical, losing the possibility of loving our enemies and even ourselves. Finally, in practicing suspicion we may lose sight of grace, God's ever-present help in forgiving us and creating within us a clean heart. As so often, it is the hymn writer who comes to our aid:

> Not for our sins alone thy mercy, Lord, we sue;
> let fall thy pitying glance on our devotions too,
> what we have done for thee, and what we think to do.
> The holiest hours we spend in prayer upon our knees,
> the times when most we deem our songs of praise will please,
> thou searcher of all hearts, forgiveness pour on these.
> And all the gifts we bring, and all the vows we make,
> and all the acts of love we plan for thy dear sake,
> into thy pard'ning thought, O God in mercy take.
> Bow down thine ear and hear! Open thine eyes and see.
> Our very love is shame, and we must come to thee
> to make it of thy grace what thou wouldst have it be.[13]

---

13. Twells, "Not For Our Sins Alone," stanzas 1–3, 5.

9

Bog Psalm

BRANDI GENTRY

An early medieval Christian Psalter was discovered in an Irish bog in 2006.

The sun cuts through bog mist like a backhoe
as rusty lichens labor beside the oxidizing sheen
of swamp water and silicate for their possessions,
rocks knobbed as skulls, and a dead deer
whose rack claws from the peat
like fingers through air.

Yet this Psalm, heavy in velum,
seems to rise from the mire,
barely eaten by the bog's dogged acid.
Inscribed by a thousand-year-old monk,
who lost it there, perhaps thinking of God's
periodic silence when arrested by the hush
surrounding this mossy sore, the parchment

climbs like a slow crack up a wall. It drags
veined pages, its bowed spine,
up alongside sphagnum and tannin
like bones covered in song.

10

"God Is Dead" and I Don't Feel So Good Myself

PETER CANDLER

While You Were Away

Taking a vacation—a proper vacation, away from cell phones, television, and newspapers—is an important thing for people to do, and for some reason, academics and Europeans seem to do it a great deal. Leisure, as readers of Aristotle's *Ethics* will recall, is the necessary condition for that most human (and for Aristotle, divine) of activities: contemplation. It is when we are free from such mundane cares that we can have the freedom to understand and experience the fullness of our humanity. The relief from the ordinary drudgery of human industry in late modernity enables us to attend not simply to the transient things of this world but to eternal truth. For those of us who cannot practice contemplation in our daily lives, a vacation may be a kind of resistance against the idolatry of what the present pope in his memoirs refers to as the "the cult of the spade."[1] And this is precisely the role of the university: to provide the space for such leisure in order that we might contemplate truth.

Of course, a vacation is not always characterized by leisure, but the ability to vacate well, to practice leisure—not just on holiday but as a matter of habit—is a great moral skill. One could appeal here to the notion, in Josef Pieper's great phrase, of leisure as the "basis of culture,"[2] or refer to the sense in which Proverbs speaks of creation in terms of Play,[3] or suggest

1. Ratzinger, *Milestones*, 33.
2. Pieper, *Leisure*.
3. Proverbs 8:27–32 (Douay-Rheims): "When he prepared the heavens, I was present:

how one may glimpse an analogy of the ordering of creation to the vision of God in the way that kittens or babies play. But returning from a vacation also teaches one a great moral lesson. If you practice a certain kind of technological asceticism when you are on vacation, which is a very big *if* in these days of Twitter, Facebook, and other kindred diversions, and if, upon your return home you happen to read the newspaper, you will very likely discover that a great deal has happened since you left. There are certain things you can probably bank on: civil unrest in the Middle East, politicians engaging in an endless game of one-upmanship, a frenzy over the state and future of global financial markets, and of course, some Hollywood starlet getting arrested for "antisocial behavior."

But more seriously, returning home from a vacation might teach us something very important about life: the world, whether we like it or not, regardless of what we have to say about it, and in spite of our most vigorous protests against it, will go on without us. Fortuna, as the ancients used to say, continues to roll on its indifferent way, and dull-witted is the mortal, says Boethius, who attempts "to stay the force of her turning wheel."[4]

One of the ways in which thinkers have responded to this set of circumstances is by recourse to some notion of "the eternal recurrence of the same," that life is nothing but the same damn thing over and over again, and then you die. There is, it must be said, considerable support for this view. It is, after all, not an entirely recent idea. The ancient Greek tragedians and epic poets may be said, in the main, to have held some version of this view; they believed that the relationship between free human choosing and the indiscriminate determinations of fate is more or less unintelligible to us, and even the gods must yield to fate's inexorable fiat. It is perhaps no accident that such a sentiment is often framed by the experience of inexplicable suffering or violence. In some cases, this view appears in the form of protest, perhaps nowhere more famously than in

---

when with a certain law and compass he enclosed the depths: When he established the sky above, and poised the fountains of waters: When he compassed the sea with its bounds, and set a law to the waters that they should not pass their limits: when he balanced the foundations of the earth; I was with him forming all things: and was delighted every day, playing before him at all times; Playing in the world: and my delights were to be with the children of men." In the Vulgate (vv. 30–31): *Cum eo eram cuncta conponens et delectabar per singulos dies ludens coram eo omni tempore ludens in orbe terrarum et deliciae meae esse cum filiis hominum.*

4. Quoting from the English translation by Villiers in Boethius, *Consolation of Philosophy*, 28 (II.1 11.59–60).

Shakespeare's *Macbeth*, where after Macbeth hears of his wife's suicide, he says:

> Tomorrow, and tomorrow, and tomorrow,
> Creeps in the petty place from day to day,
> To the last syllable of recorded time;
> And all our yesterdays have lighted fools
> The way to dusty death. Out, out, brief candle,
> Life's but a walking shadow, a poor player
> That struts and frets his hour upon the stage,
> And then is heard no more. It is a tale
> Told by an idiot, full of sound and fury
> Signifying nothing.[5]

Speaking of "signifying nothing," some journalists, pop sociologists, politicians, and other cultural theorists tell us that one of the more surprising historical developments at the end of the twentieth century has been the return of religion, and with it, the dramatically increased influence of religious groups upon world affairs. Witness, for example, the recent political battles over the massive voting power of so-called American evangelicals—both Democrats and Republicans in the current climate compete with one another over the authenticity of their religious faith and their ability to speak the language of religion, not to mention disgraced public figures suddenly finding Jesus, bong hits for Christ, and so on.

It doesn't take a cynic to say that:

> Disillusioned words like bullets bark
> As human gods aim for their mark
> Made everything from toy guns that spark
> To flesh-colored Christs that glow in the dark
> It's easy to see without looking too far
> That not much
> Is really sacred.[6]

It should come as little surprise, then, to find some denizens of the publishing world seizing upon this moment in which religion has made a

5. Shakespeare, *Macbeth*, V.v, 19–28 (p. 105).
6. Dylan, "It's Alright, Ma (I'm Only Bleeding)."

so-called comeback. A handful of books that have appeared over the past couple of years suggest that the newfound religious fervor of Westerners is an entirely pernicious phenomenon. Books like Sam Harris's *Letter to a Christian Nation*, Richard Dawkins's *The God Delusion*, and Christopher Hitchens's *God Is Not Great: How Religion Poisons Everything*, each, in their own way, argue that religion is the source of all evil in the world, and therefore, once we abolish it, we may return to the benighted vision of the secular civil society. The French philosopher Michel Onfray has recently pressed the case still further: in his *Atheist Manifesto*, he argues for a secularism that is post-Christian, purged of its latent and residually Judeo-Christian ethics of toleration and intellectual generosity. So he is as opposed to relativism as he is to the Judeo-Christian inheritance, because they are both genealogically related. Hence, the stirring rhetoric of the conclusion to his manifesto:

> At this hour when the final battle—already lost—looms for the defense of the Enlightenment's values against magical proposi- tions, we must fight for a post-Christian secularism, that is to say, atheistic, militant, and radically opposed to choosing between Western Judeo-Christianity and its Islamic adversary—neither Bible nor Koran. I persist in preferring philosophers to rabbis, priests, imams, ayatollahs, and mullahs. Rather than trust their theological hocus-pocus, I prefer to draw on alternatives to the dominant philosophical historiography: the laughers, material- ists, radicals, cynics, hedonists, atheists, sensualists, voluptuaries. They know that there is only one world, and that promotion of an afterlife deprives us of the enjoyment and benefit of the only one there is.[7]

I need not go further into the various arguments—if we may call them that—of these four books, and in some ways your leisure might be better spent in other pursuits. Perhaps I should count myself among the laughers and cynics in Onfray's manifesto, for there is certainly much in his own case—as well as in those of Harris, Dawkins, and Hitchens—to laugh at, were it not so depressingly theologically and philosophically illiterate.

Suffice it to say that if this gang of atheists represents the highest form of atheism these days, and if every atheism is always parasitic upon some form of theism, then the critiques of religion offered in these books

7. Onfray, *Atheist Manifesto*, 219.

imply that the state of theology in public discourse is pretty dismal. Granted, these kinds of books are products of a multibillion-dollar industry, and although they do not represent the cutting edge of scholarship, their popularity does seem to confirm this basic point: in spite of what we are told about the resurgence of religion, particularly in American life, perhaps now more than ever, it is next to impossible to talk about God intelligently in the public square. This intellectual miasma is enough to make one pine for the days when there were atheists around of the stature and philosophical integrity of Nietzsche. But, after all, every age gets the atheism it deserves.[8]

One problem with these books is that they may encourage us not to take our opponents very seriously—indeed, it is often a work of immense intellectual generosity to take the rhetoric of Harris, Dawkins, Hitchens, and Onfray very seriously. If anything, these books conceal from us what there is genuinely to learn from good atheism. For there is a distinction between good atheism and bad. The aforementioned texts are examples of the bad variety; the work of Nietzsche is an example of the beneficent variety. Nietzsche may have been guilty, as David Hart has suggested, of having "atrocious taste," nevertheless "[w]here Nietzsche is most convincing, and where his treatment of Christianity cannot be factually gainsaid, is where he portrays the church's faith as a telling of the tale of being to which he is implacably opposed, in place of which he intends to tell another story." His thought remains, for all that, "quite close to theology."[9]

At some profound level, Nietzsche seems to have understood Christianity in a way that many Christians of his own age did not. Even if the God whose death he proclaimed was really an idol, the product of a decadent metaphysics, Nietzsche nonetheless recognized the centrality of the Christian event to European culture in general and to philosophy in particular. He understood that its displacement required an utterly new story, and for Nietzsche that story is one of conflict and will-to-power. In other words, once the Christian God has died, he must be replaced with something else.

If there is any benefit to be found in such good atheism, it is in its iconoclasm, or better yet, its idoloclasm. Good atheism might help to expose our conceptions of God, the cosmos, and ourselves as idolatrous; the

8. I owe this line to Michael Hanby.

9. Hart, *Beauty of the Infinite*, 125, 117, 93.

objects of our belief as a fiction; the source of our faith as, for example, fear and self-love rather than proper charity; and the object and source of all knowledge as some finite idol rather than the Triune God.

Given this iconoclasm, it is no accident that the new story that Nietzsche tells is the same one that I mentioned earlier: there is really nothing new in the universe, and the only way to survive is through the naked embrace of the will-to-power. As Henri de Lubac correctly states, "The Eternal Return is imperative as the indispensable substitute for a dead God. It alone can seal up the stone of his tomb."[10]

For Nietzsche, the death of God resulted in a total transformation of reality. Consider the way in which Nietzsche himself described the scene of the crime, in that oft-quoted passage from *The Gay Science,* which has virtually become the testament of our times:

> Have you not heard of that madman who lit a lantern in the bright morning hours, ran to the market place, and cried incessantly: "I seek God! I seek God!"—As many of those who did not believe in God were standing around just then, he provoked much laughter. Has he got lost? asked one. Did he lose his way like a child? asked another. Or is he hiding? Is he afraid of us? Has he gone on a voyage? Emigrated?
>
> . . . The madman jumped into their midst and pierced them with his eyes. "Whither is God," he cried; "I will tell you. *We have killed him*—you and I. All of us are his murderers. . . . Are we not straying as through infinite nothing? Do we not feel the breath of empty space? Has it not become colder? . . . Do we hear nothing as yet of the noise of the gravediggers who are burying God? Do we smell nothing as yet of the divine decomposition? Gods, too, decompose. God is dead. God remains dead. And we have killed him.
>
> ". . . There has never been a greater deed; and whoever is born after us—for the sake of this deed he will belong to a higher history than all history hitherto."
>
> Here the madman fell silent and looked again at his listeners; and they too were silent and stared at him in astonishment. At last he threw his lantern on the ground, and it broke into pieces and went out. "I have come too early," he said then; "My time is not yet. This tremendous event is still on its way, . . . still more distant from them than the most distant stars—*and yet they have done it themselves.*

10. Lubac, *Drama of Atheist Humanism,* 496.

> ... [O]n the same day the madman forced his way into sev-
> eral churches and there struck up his *requiem aeternam deo*. Led
> out and called to account, he is said always to have replied noth-
> ing but: "What after all are these churches now if they are not the
> tombs and sepulcher of God?"[11]

Rather than a prophet who announces what shall yet come to pass, Nietzsche's madman is a seer who recognizes the despair into which the world is hurled at this "greatest recent event." That is to say, the annunciation of the death of God is not a *performative* utterance—it does not enact what it announces; rather, the proclamation is a declaration of the way things appear to be. That is, for Nietzsche, the utterance "God is dead" is a cultural claim: God is dead in the sense that he is no longer of use to us. The modern, scientific world has no need of God to explain the mysteries of the world. Everything, so the argument goes, can be accounted for by means of the language of the natural sciences. On this account, Nietzsche is hardly the father of a nihilistic age; rather, he writes as one born into the era of European nihilism, and his entire philosophy is, in essence, an attempt to overcome this nihilism.

"God is dead" is a declaration that a world without God is a world in peril, a declaration that a world which believes itself finally free of God can no longer live in the same manner it had previously. Now everything must be overturned. Nothing will be the same. With the death of God, the "entire horizon" is "wipe[d] away," the "earth is unchained from its sun," "plunging continually" in every direction and in no direction. As such, all evaluative structures are destroyed, even the designation of direction— "Is there still any up or down?" The world living in the shadow of God will be one of utter confusion, a world in which men carry lanterns into the marketplace when it is an already bright morning, a world in which the wisest among us are pronounced mad.

However, it is important to notice that in this passage Nietzsche is not unreservedly celebrating the death of God. He resists situating himself either on the side of devastated mourning or exuberant celebration. There remains an unresolved tension in his proclamation that desists from qualitative appraisal of this "greatest recent event." Instead, he acknowledges the tension between utter tragedy and relieved gaiety. Nietzsche is unable to exult in the death of God because he is acutely aware of the inevitable

---

11. Nietzsche, *Gay Science*, section 125 (p. 181–82).

consequences it will have for the future. Thus, his project of the revaluation of all values is born. Regardless of one's reaction to God's death, there is no possibility for complacent indifference. Rather, Nietzsche himself realizes the extent to which the future of history is "for the sake of this deed" fraught with horrific magnitude. As such, "His insight that 'God is dead' imposes an inexorable task upon him."[12] This task is summarized several sections before the famous parable of the madman; Nietzsche writes:

> After Buddha was dead, his shadow was still shown for centuries in a cave—a tremendous, gruesome shadow. God is dead; but given the way of men, there may still be caves for thousands of years in which his shadow will be shown—And we—we still have to vanquish his shadow, too.[13]

Everything Is Broken

In John Updike's 1996 novel, *In the Beauty of the Lilies*, Clarence Wilmot is the pastor of a small Presbyterian congregation in the town of Paterson, New Jersey, just across the Passaic River from the sprawling metropolis of New York City. In response to the questions of a skeptical member of his church, Wilmot begins reading the "masters of suspicion"—Ingersoll, Hume, Darwin, Renan, Nietzsche—[14] in order to adequately and learnedly counter and refute the suspicions of his querulous parishioner. However, in the course of his research, Wilmot finds himself succumbing to the very suspicion he is attempting to combat. As a result, he loses his faith, resigns his ministry, and leaves the church, eventually taking a new job as an encyclopedia salesman and becoming an avid moviegoer. At one point, Updike writes, "He could not tell her how even pronouncing words had become a heaviness, now that the true nature of reality was revealed. *There is no God.* Perhaps everybody, back to his professors at Princeton, had known it already."[15]

---

12. Jaspers, *Nietzsche*, 247.

13. Nietzsche, *Gay Science*, section 108 (p. 167).

14. Updike, *In the Beauty of the Lilies*, 40.

15. Ibid., 60.

Updike makes reference here to college professors, particularly Ivy League professors, as bearing the secret truth of things: God is dead, and we theologians have known it all along. This is a variation on the old theme—go to college an innocent Christian and leave a jaded atheist. In fact, a professor of philosophy in Texas has written a book entitled *How to Stay Christian in College*. It is worth asking what such a title—if not the text itself—presumes.

The landscape painted by Updike is one in which the death of God is more or less an obvious fact of the modern world (the story begins in 1910), and perhaps more than anything else, the modern university. The phenomenon of modern atheism is so pervasive that the death of God is not something that needs to be announced. It is, for those who find themselves unable to celebrate it, like a dark cloud that hangs over Western culture, blotting out all suns, threatening all of life with utter loss of significance. Like the men and women in the marketplace in Nietzsche's parable of the madman, citizens of the West act as though God were dead, but they appear not to perceive the true significance of this fact: "The problem with atheism is that it is not a problem. It is a situation, an atmosphere, a confused history whose assertions can be identical in expression and positively contradictory in sense."[16]

Similarly, Nicholas Lash likens the "situation" in contemporary Christianity to an airport departure lounge, a "restless space in which a continuously shifting crowd of strangers mingles, somewhat nervously, against a background of piped music and occasional obscure commands." It is an atmosphere that lacks any real "centre of activity, giving purpose and direction to the whole"; indeed, the fact that the group of inhabitants of the airport lounge is never the same, nor even close to the same, is suggestive of the fact that there appears to be no real "whole" to speak of: the fragmentation of our world runs so deep that this seems to us to be all there is.[17] The death of God is, as René Girard writes, "the Pavlovian reflex of modernity."[18]

The fragmentation of not just contemporary Christianity but of Western society in general could be attributed in part to the loss of a single unifying narrative constitutive of a community's identity, which

16. Buckley, *At the Origins of Modern Atheism*, 13.
17. Lash, "Among Strangers and Friends," 53.
18. Girard, "Founding Murder in the Philosophy of Nietzsche," 232.

the tumultuous years of "religious" wars in the mid-seventeenth century made only more confusing and disjointed. The seventeenth and eighteenth centuries' quest for certainty attempted to resolve this confusion and widespread disagreement by virtue of a disinterested arbitrator, namely in the form of a universal, indubitable "Reason." The Christian narrative of history, which had unified medieval Christendom, was gradually displaced from its central position, and Reason, now sundered from faith, left the two realms on opposite sides of a chasm across which there is no commerce. As Maurice Blondel writes:

> [W]hen reason, left sole mistress of the knowable world, claimed to find immanent in herself all the truths needed for the life of man, the world of faith found itself totally excluded: juxtaposition led to opposition and incompatibility.[19]

In place of the complex interrelation of reason and faith characteristic of the Middle Ages, the modern world set the totalizing metanarrative of scientific rationality, which sought to unify all forms of knowledge and discourse under the universally objective mode of Reason. The failure of the modern world's attempts at a synthesizing grand theory has resulted in the seemingly endless fracturing of academic disciplines, not to mention the fragmentation of what were once genuine human communities into the mere aggregates of independent, atomistic individuals. What was once a source of much optimism—a new reign of Reason that would ultimately quell all doubt and dissolve all disagreement—has given way to a general unease, if not mutiny, as it has become clear that the hopes for a benevolent regime of Reason are ill-placed. Stephen Toulmin rather succinctly sums up the atmosphere of late or post-modernity thus:

> Today, the program of Modernity—even the very concept—no longer carries anything like the same conviction. If an historical era is ending, it is the era of Modernity itself. Rather than our being free to assume that the tide of Modernity still flows strongly, and that its momentum will carry us into a new and better world, our present position is less comfortable. What looked in the nineteenth century like an irresistible river has disappeared in the sand, and we seem to have run aground. Far from extrapolating

19. Blondel, "Letter on Apologetics," 148.

confidently into the social and cultural future, we are now stranded
and uncertain of our location.[20]

This breaking up of Western culture is due not least of all to the West's
loss of the Christian story as that which constitutes its identity. The aim-
lessness of Lash's airport lounge is simply indicative, or symbolic, of the
loss of the modern West's identity. There was perhaps no better critical
diagnostician of the pathology of post-Christian man than Walker Percy,
who wrote that "The present age is demented. It is possessed by a sense
of dislocation, a loss of personal identity, an alternating sentimentality and rage which, in an individual patient, could be characterized as
dementia."[21] Similarly, Percy's contemporary, Flannery O'Connor, once
said famously, "This is a generation of wingless chickens, which I suppose
is what Nietzsche meant when he said God was dead."[22]

What is curious about Updike's story is the extent to which the widespread loss of belief, the loss of the *possibility* of faith in "God," results
in a total and complete reversal of everything; every human activity, no
matter how petty or mundane, must be reevaluated; all the structures for
evaluating and assessing what is true and what is false are called into question. Indeed, Updike's preacher recognizes this when even "pronouncing
words" becomes for him a matter of "heaviness." In a world in which such
minute aspects of human activity already possess profound significance
(that is, in the world before the death of God), is such a radical upheaval
of "values" possible, indeed required? In a world such as ours, where it is
virtually taken for granted that these actions possess little or no qualitative merit, such a loss of identity would, I dare say, go unnoticed.

Consider a rather more inventive way of putting the matter: in *The
Amber Spyglass*, the third volume of Philip Pullman's fantasy trilogy, His
Dark Materials, Pullman as it were re-enacts the death of God:

> Between them they helped the ancient of days out of his crystal
> cell; it wasn't hard, for he was as light as paper, and he would
> have followed them anywhere, having no will of his own, and

20. Toulmin, *Cosmopolis*, 3.

21. Percy, "Why Are You a Catholic?" 309. My title, which I confess to having ripped
from another great Southern writer, the columnist Lewis Grizzard, is intended in the
Percyan spirit; Grizzard was, however, not bemoaning God's death, but Elvis's (sometimes, especially in parts of the South, it is difficult to know the difference.)

22. O'Connor, *Habit of Being*, 90.

responding to simple kindness like a flower to the sun. But in the open air there was nothing to stop the wind from damaging him, and to their dismay his form began to loosen and dissolve. Only a few moments later he had vanished completely, and their last impression was of those eyes, blinking in wonder, and a sigh of the most profound and exhausted relief.

Then he was gone: a mystery dissolving in mystery.[23]

This goes a step farther than Nietzsche, in at least one sense. Whereas Nietzsche's proclamation of the death of the old God is somewhat problematic, Pullman's narrative is one in which God's vanishing is the occasion for profound relief, even gratitude. The "ancient of days" is grateful to humanity for his liberation, his final freedom for self-annihilation. I wonder if Pullman doesn't capture a peculiar kind of modern theological apathy, according to which we are not only done with God, but God is glad to be done with us—moreover, God is glad to be done with himself.

But at another level, the conclusion of *The Amber Spyglass* once again repeats a familiar theme; in a kind of Voltairean flourish at the end of the novel, we are left with the responsibility to build—this time not the Kingdom, but the Republic of Heaven. Once again, as with the other denizens of popular atheism, there is a call for a return to the Enlightenment and its great values of liberty, equality, and fraternity. These are all noble values, to be sure, but to what or to whom, in the absence of God, are we left to owe our allegiance, nay, our adoration? In each case, this object of adoration is invariably the modern secular state, which alone, the argument goes, can guarantee those values and ensure us a civilization free of violence.

It is no accident that one of the backdrops for Pullman's trilogy—and there are many, for this work traverses a great multiplicity of worlds—is the University of Oxford, home to the main character, the semi-orphan Lyra, and her parents, who find themselves on opposite sides of the struggle to understand dust. And it is no mere coincidence that Updike's protagonist's loss of faith is occasioned by studies at Princeton. The presupposition seems to be that if you think hard about it, if you really use your mind, then faith will be exposed as illusion, superstition, even a lie. Faith, it is presumed, simply cannot survive the university life.

23. Pullman, *Amber Spyglass*, 410–11.

When I lived in Durham, North Carolina, I remember one day walking across the Duke University campus, and I noticed that someone had written, in huge chalk letters in front of Duke Chapel, the words, "How can we think freely in the shadow of a chapel?" At first blush, it might seem a good question, but really, it is not entirely clear the question is all that intelligible.

Yet the presupposition is plainly there, and it's all too common: we can't think clearly until the shadow of God has finally and decisively been vanquished, when the pathetic, fear-engendering spirit of religion has been exorcised, when, finally, we have freed God from the world. For in so doing, we ourselves will begin to glimpse our own liberty at first light.

So the story goes, anyway.

It's interesting, I think, to notice that Pullman replaces the notion of kingdom with the notion of republic, and in their own way, so do the other atheist critics I have mentioned. But why are there only two models of human community to choose from? Might this be an example of the extent to which reason and faith's divorce has left their children homeless and our imaginations orphaned? Are there any other possibilities for imagining human community?

The lectionary readings from the feast of Saint Augustine of Hippo all touch on a metaphor familiar and dear to his heart: the city of God, the *civitas dei*. In his book of the same title, Augustine famously deconstructed, as it were, the logic of the earthly city, showing it to be premised upon the necessity of violence, the worship of the tragic, the praise of war. In contrast, Augustine said, there is another city:

> You have come to Mount Zion and to the city of the living God, the heavenly Jerusalem, and to innumerable angels in festal gathering, and to the assembly of the firstborn who are enrolled in heaven, and to God the judge of all, and to the spirits of the righteous made perfect, and to Jesus, the mediator of a new covenant, and to the sprinkled blood that speaks a better word than the blood of Abel. Therefore, since we are receiving a kingdom that cannot be shaken, let us give thanks, by which we offer to God an acceptable worship with reverence and awe; for indeed our God is a consuming fire. (Heb 12:22–24; 12:28–29)

Augustine writes of a city and a kingdom, to be sure, maybe even a republic, but it is one whose logic is peace and whose law is charity, not the mere suspension of violence.

Let me indulge in a speculative exercise for a moment. There is at least one other model of human social life that is neither a city, a kingdom, nor a republic. It is a form of life with its origins in the Christian Middle Ages, and it is quite possibly the most universal institution in the world, apart from the Roman Catholic Church. It is the university.

My good friend Michael Hanby points out that the university in its original constitution assumed one thing at least: the existence of a universe, a world of intelligible reality, which, through the faithful and disciplined exercise of our minds and in response to Christ's call to love the Lord God with all our heart, all our soul, and all our mind (Matt 22:37), we could—in some measure, however incomplete—understand.

The late Luigi Giussani, in his book *The Risk of Education,* argues:

> The Christian fact is permanent throughout history. It has a structure that nothing can change because it is a definitive event. Nevertheless, the Christian who lives out this event, in dealing with the cultural, social, and political conditions of his times— unless he lacks intelligence or is totally slothful—cannot help but judge the prevailing ideas and structures from the point of view of his lived faith. As a result, the desire to create an alternative culture and alternative structure is unavoidable.[24]

I trust that this readership lacks neither intelligence nor industry, so it is for those with memory, the intellect and will, to imagine what such an alternative intellectual culture might look like.

The divorce of reason and faith has left us without a universe. Moreover, in the interest of preserving their integrity, the divorce proceedings have left both parties bitter and no longer on speaking terms. In the process, we have left everything in fragments. But if we are to imagine, in the spirit of Saint Augustine, a university of a very different kind—*a universitas dei,* if I may—it can only be one informed by the story of the world according to which the fragments of five loaves fill twelve baskets, in which the story of Christian faith informs the heights and the depths of our intellectual life and work. In every discipline, therefore, it remains

24. Giussani, *Risk of Education,* 117.

for us to unlearn the atheism of our own thought, which is another way of saying, "take every thought captive to Christ" (2 Cor 10:5).

Augustine famously described faith as seeking understanding (*quaerens intellectum*). The university, then, provides us the leisure to be restless for such understanding, to restlessly seek the God in whom true rest is found. Many college campuses lack a chapel big enough to cast such a hopeful shadow, but if anything, thinking in shadows ought not to be something foreign to Christians, who "see now as in a glass darkly." It is therefore the luminous darkness of the Christian mystery that does not put an end to but marks the beginning of our reason's true vocation. For as Augustine himself says, "Unthinking faith is nothing."[25]

25. Augustine *De Praedestinatione Sanctorum* II.5: « *uoniam fides si non cogitetur, nulla est.* »

11

Reading Philip Pullman in Metro Manila

Andy Barnes

Taho is a kind of watery yogurt made from bean curd. That didn't sound good to me, but my wife's eyes went wide when she heard the vendor calling. It's a favorite with Filipino children, and she'd left Manila when she was eight. The vendor was carrying two big buckets on a yoke across his shoulders, with the bean curd in one bucket and water in the other. He mixed them together in a plastic cup, and we paid him a few cents. The watery curd looked unappetizing, to say the least, but I had a bite, and it tasted better than it looked. This experience was unpleasantly inverted when I visited the slums in Quezon City.

From the outside, the neighborhood looked nice enough. Like so many other places in Metro Manila, there were rows of white two-story houses pressed together against narrow streets, but when we walked down an alley and then turned into a dark passageway, I found a different way of living. There was a labyrinth of tunnels filled with low doorways. I had to bend my back, and the ground was uneven and covered with puddles of grime. There were places where the shacks gave way to patches of sky, and rainwater ran off tin roofs into buckets. Other places were so dark that it took an act of faith to step forward, and as my eyes adjusted, I saw that there were children everywhere, many of them without shoes, and all of them too thin. I saw a girl washing herself with filthy water that was white like milk, and I was told that more than twenty families use a single latrine.

The owners of the slums are also the owners of the taho factory. The vendors live here, and they set out every morning to sell the taho and earn a couple of dollars. They pay almost half of their earnings back to the factory owners for the dubious privilege of living in their slums.

Our guide was a volunteer with an evangelical group that provides scholarships for children who would otherwise have to drop out of school. Some of the people in the slum knew the volunteer and were eager to talk to him.

We came to a doorway filled with light, and a man invited us into a room only a few yards wide, a room where his entire family lived. There was a counter with old wooden cabinets under it, and on the cabinets were large, printed animals, dancing bears in clothes or something, like old *Golden Books* characters. The image was out of place, and I felt disoriented.

Someone pulled up a stool and told me to sit. A baby slept in a blanket that hung from the ceiling, and a girl who might have been eight lay on the floor in the corner. We'd woken her up. She'd been sleeping on the hard floor with a single small pillow under her head. She stared at me, and she didn't smile like all the other kids I'd met in the Philippines. I stared back.

Call it the Anne Frank effect. There was no way for me to get my mind around the suffering I was seeing, so I fixated on a single child and identified with her. It's like when Lewis points out that no single person has to endure all the suffering of humanity, and so God has spread the problem of pain so thin we can almost swallow it.[1]

Her older sister appeared in the doorway, and our guide told me that the organization was paying for the older girl to be in school and if she did well, they'd send her to college. Classrooms and books seemed so far away from that little room where the whole family sleeps on top of each other.

A couple weeks later, we were back in Quezon City visiting a home for abused girls that was run by Salesian Sisters. In the van on the way, one of the sisters turned around in the front seat and told us in direct, unflinching terms about the lives these girls led in the slums. She described the limited sleeping space, the lack of privacy, and the conditions that lead to abuse. When we arrived, the girls lined up and sang a song, complete with hand motions. It was a song asking Jesus why children

---

1. Lewis, *Problem of Pain*, 116.

have to suffer. Their faces were sad while they sang and happy again when they'd finished.

While I was in the Philippines, I happened to be reading the last two books of Philip Pullman's His Dark Materials trilogy. I'd approached the series with some ambivalence the month before because, although I knew Pullman was anti-Christian, anti-Lewis, and anti-Tolkien, Pullman was a part of the Oxford tradition I learned to love, having been raised on Lewis, Tolkien, and Alice.

When I met Lyra in the first chapters of *The Golden Compass*, I was immediately drawn to her character and to her world, and by the end of the first book, I was confused, because I wasn't seeing much of an anti-religious message. The villains in *The Golden Compass* are unethical, power-hungry scientists, who seem to have stepped out of Lewis's space trilogy. Sure, the good witches of the books are sanctimonious culture-war feminists, and the religious types are neurotic, genuflecting sadists, but what are a few straw men between a good reader and a good story?

Unfortunately, both the tone of the books and my perspective shifted in Manila. I knew things were heading downhill when I came to a passage in *The Subtle Knife*, wherein a witch makes the following speech:

> "Sisters," she began, "let me tell you what is happening, and who it is that we must fight. For there is a war coming. I don't know who will join with us, but I know whom we must fight. It is the Magisterium, the Church. For all its history—and that's not long by their lives, but it is many, many of theirs—it's tried to suppress and control every natural impulse. And when it can't control them, it cuts them out. Some of you have seen what they did at Bolvanger. And that was horrible, but it is not the only such place, not the only such practice. Sisters, you know only the north; I have traveled in the southlands. There are churches there, believe me, that cut their children too—as the people in Bolvanger did—not in the same way, but just as horribly. They cut their sexual organs, yes, both boys and girls; they cut them with knives so that they shan't feel. That is what the Church does, and every church is the same: destroy, control, obliterate every good feeling. So if a war comes, and the Church is on one side of it, we must be on the other, no matter what strange allies we find ourselves bound to."[2]

2. Pullman, *Subtle Knife*, 44–45.

In Pullman's world, the church isn't just to be held accountable for its own sins, but the sins of all other religions and all a-religions as well. Everything from female genital mutilation to Dr. Mengele are on the side of Christ, while what is "natural" and "good" is on the side of the witches and the heroes of the books.

I've noticed that the word *natural* is a kind of magic word for many people. It's used as if what is natural is perfectly obvious, objective, self-evident, and good, but what is considered good in human society is not directly evident in nature—after all, no one seems to argue that we should behave more like animals. There is no obvious, objective, self-evident understanding of what natural means. And discussions about what is natural are ongoing debates about what is good, and it's clear that there is overlap in what Pullman, the witches, and Christians would consider good and natural. As a Christian, I too would be horrified by the experiments conducted on the children in *The Golden Compass* and—on a much more serious level—I'm horrified by female genital mutilation in northern Africa. Does Pullman believe it's unnatural, evil, and oppressive when an evangelical NGO goes into the slums and provides the means for educating some of Metro Manila's poorest children, or does he believe it's wrong of the Salesian Sisters to work every day, sacrificing families of their own, to provide abused girls with a safe home? And if he doesn't see these services as wrong, then why reduce the entire question of morality to such inadequate terms? Why call out the church, and every religious person on the planet, and then offer up such a thin argument?

The Filipino Christians I met in Quezon City, both Protestant and Catholic, approach the slums with a clear message: What we do in this life matters, because God created us for a purpose. Sins can be forgiven, and there is a better life beyond the grave. In one of their schools, the Salesian Sisters had a banner that read, "Heaven Is My Destiny." I might have snickered at such a nakedly sentimental statement, but the teenagers who were standing under the banner were so obviously happy. They had found hope in a very dark place; belief in another life gave them the strength to succeed in this life.

The comfort Pullman offers in his books is depressingly insufficient. His idea, if I understand him correctly, is that people have souls that are made of dark matter. These dark-matter souls can be separated from a person's material body and held together in a ghost-like form, but this separation is unnatural and undesirable. The preferred fate is atomization of both body and soul so that the atoms can spread out across the universe and serve as material for new life forms. We've all heard this circle-of-life idea before, of course, and I've never understood the attraction. Why should a zebra be happy to sacrifice his body to lions? Should soldiers killed in war be happy to sacrifice themselves to the victors? Would cannibalism make their sacrifice more meaningful?

Here's Pullman on the glory of atomization:

> We'll be alive again in a thousand blades of grass, and a million leaves; we'll be falling in the raindrops and blowing in the fresh breeze; we'll be glittering in the dew under the stars and the moon. . . . We'll live in birds and flowers and dragonflies and pine trees and in clouds and in those little specks of light you see floating in sunbeams. . . . All the atoms all the living things. [We'll] never vanish. [We'll] just [be] part of everything. And that's exactly what'll happen to [us], I swear to you, I promise on my honor. [We'll] drift apart, it's true, but [we'll] be out in the open, part of everything, alive again. . . . And when the battle's over, there'll be all the time in the world to drift along the wind and find the atoms that used to be [our friends], and [our] mother[s] in the sagelands, and [our] sweethearts—all [our] sweethearts.[3]

Shakespeare's Hamlet contemplates atomization with different results:

> Hamlet: Why, may not imagination trace the noble dust of Alexander till a find it stopping a bung-hole? . . . Alexander died, Alexander was buried, Alexander returneth to dust, the dust is earth, of earth we make loam, and why of that loam whereto he was converted might they not stop a beer-barrel?

> Imperious Caesar, dead and turn'd to clay,
> Might stop a hole to keep the wind away.
> O that that earth which kept the world in awe
> Should patch a wall t'expel the winter's flaw.[4]

And again, with a bit more venom:

> King: Now, Hamlet, where's Polonius?

---

3. Pullman, *Amber Spyglass*, 320; 497; 319; and 385.

4. Shakespeare, *Hamlet*, V.i, 196–98 and 201–10.

Hamlet: At supper.

King: At supper? Where?

Hamlet: Not where he eats, but where he is eaten. A certain con-vocation of politic worms are e'en at him. Your worm is your only emperor for diet: we fat all creatures else to fat us, and we fat our-selves for maggots. Your fat king and your lean beggar is but vari-able service—two dishes, but to one table. That's the end.

King: Alas, alas.

Hamlet: A man may fish with the worm that hath eat of a king, and eat of the fish that hath fed of that worm.

King: What dost thou mean by this?

Hamlet: Nothing but to show you how a king may go a progress through the guts of a beggar.[5]

But Pullman apparently doesn't get the joke. Consider the following pas-sage from *The Amber Spyglass*, written without a trace of irony, in which a sentient polar bear devours the corpse of his cowboy friend:

And because the Texan aeronaut was one of the very few humans Iorek had ever esteemed, he accepted the man's last gift to him. With deft movements of his claws, he ripped aside the dead man's clothes, opened the body with one slash, and began to feast on the flesh and blood of his old friend. It was his first meal in days, and he was hungry.[6]

So Pullman mixes descriptions of the ecstasy of spiritual atomization (af-ter death, we ride on the wind and become parts of grass and whatnot) with descriptions of the circle of life in action (after death, our corpses are meat for the devouring), and in both cases, he seems to suggest that there is meaning for the decomposed in these transactions. It almost seems too obvious to state, but Philip Pullman gets good reviews, so I will: even if there is no spiritual dimension and the human mind is made entirely of matter, an individual personality is not contained in individual atoms but in a specific, evolving arrangement of atoms. When that arrange-ment suddenly decomposes, as in death, unless there is a supernatural force that will recompose the order of those atoms or a spiritual element

5. Ibid., IV.iii, 16–31.
6. Pullman, *Amber Spyglass*, 42.

that will preserve the order in some other dimension, that individual's personality—including their self-consciousness—is gone. The individual atoms that composed the body are dust. If those atoms go on to become parts of other beings, be they lions, polar bears, or kings, no vestige of the deceased's personality will be present in that new being. If our souls are made of dark matter, and dark matter decomposes in the same way, then the result will be the same. An atom, by definition, is too fundamental a piece of matter to contain the information necessary for consciousness, and without some continuity of consciousness, we are—in every meaningful sense of the word—dead.

I'm sure these books read better in Oxford than in Manila. When you have questions in Oxford, there are books. When you are cold, there are pubs. Nature is as close as the meadows and the river. London, with all its cultural institutions, is a short bus ride away. When you're at home there, Oxford is the kind of city that leaves you space to wonder what's down rabbit holes and behind wardrobes. Don't misunderstand me, whimsy can have deadly serious ends—and the best of it always does—but it requires a delicate balance between what is real and what is imagined. There are different kinds of truth, and the best fantasy writers, like all good artists, intuitively recognize the truth that can be bent and the truth that is sacred. Tolkien and Lewis succeed because their castles are built with the stones of ancient tradition, stones that have been worn down by time to leave only the hardest material. In his zeal, Pullman atomizes these stones, and although the experiment might be interesting in a warm Oxford pub (or a warm Starbucks in Washington State), in Manila, all I see is a man trying to build castles with dust.

If there is no God, no second life, and no redemption, then there is no hope for these slums, because too much has been lost already. Everything is rising entropy, decomposition, and atomization, and there's no way to glorify that here. It would be atoms in the filthy drinking water, atoms in the smog, atoms in the glue, atoms moving in and out of people who are given no space to imagine a better life. And if these people stopped believing in Christ, and they had only atomization to look forward to, and if the church stopped sending its people with aid, then they'd have even less hope than they have now. And if a baby girl is born in a slum, lives a short life of pain and suffering, and then her body and soul decompose at her death, then from her perspective, her life is not one bit more meaningful because we write odes to her scattered atoms.

If we're of a particular frame of mind, an ode might make *us* feel better, but for the people in these slums (and for Hamlet) it would just be a sick joke that in death she is no less fortunate than a queen.

12

The Skeptic's Gospel and Other Remedies for Truth

Paul Roorda

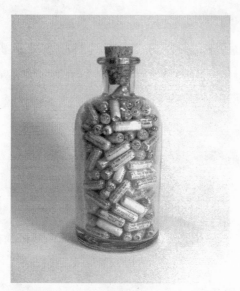

"Once Daily (New Testament)," Bible pages, gelatin capsules,
antique bottle, and cork

The Truth is elusive; it is camouflaged in dappled shadows. Instead of the black-and-white reality that I sometimes seek and imagine, I see two truths at once, and where I thought one Truth was steady before my eyes, I see no truth at all. There is a transparency to what I thought was solid, a duplicity to what I thought was one, and layered meanings where I thought I had found understanding. Ours is a world where the results change each

"Crown of Thorns and Capeline Bandage," blood, crushed stone, rust, gold leaf, beeswax, and vintage book pages on paper

"The Dead Christ and Four Bearers," blood, crushed stone, rust, gold leaf, beeswax, and vintage book pages on paper

time we perform an identical action and where we get the same result no matter what we try. And in this lovely, kaleidoscopic, paradoxically shifting world of mystery, a gospel lies waiting to be unraveled from its tightly wound spool into a tangled, looping nest of truths where the lines aren't straight and the ends cannot be found. And that is the Skeptic's Gospel.

"Small Miracle (Wine to Water)," red wine distilled and purified into water,
vintage apothecary bottle, and communion glasses

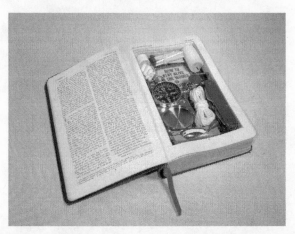

"Survival Kit for Uncertain Times," Bible, matches, candle, fishing tackle,
compass, pocket knife, mirror, whistle, string, pain killers in vial,
and wilderness survival book

"Open Bible IV (Nail Arch)," Bible with nails

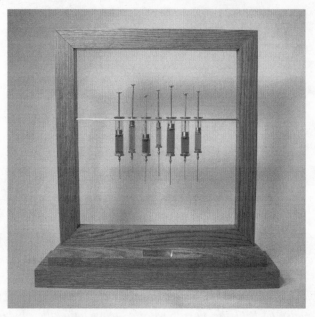

"Seven (Heavenly/Deadly)," vintage syringes, dye extracted from Gideon Bibles fermented to make wine, wood, glass, and aluminum

"Self-portrait as the Shroud of Turin," Bible pages,
wheat, smoke, and beeswax on board

13

Miltonian Rebukes in an Age of Reason: A Conversation between Stanley Fish and Stanley Hauerwas

In a 2009 *New York Times* blog entry reviewing Terry Eagleton's *Reason, Faith, and Revolution: Reflections on the God Debate*, the esteemed literary critic Stanley Fish surprised readers by dismissing the quality of the New Atheist polemics and revealing something of a disdain for the character of the New Atheist brood. His defense of religion, however, proved too inclusive for the progressive *New York Times* readership, and hundreds of readers wrote in to challenge his seemingly irrational religious sympathies. They wrote with vitriol and exasperation, questioning how Fish could make sympathetic claims for faith in the face of such objective scientific advancement. Fish responded with a second blog entry that delved deeper into the anatomy of these arguments, reminding the good readers of the *Times* that observations cannot exist in a vacuum, that we are always observing while tethered to a larger system of beliefs, ergo, the scientist is not quite the calculated observer he claims to be. This entry, too, garnered hundreds of comments (797 at last count), many of them angry—Stanley Fish was hitting a nerve.

Shortly after these blog posts were published, Fish agreed to talk further about atheism with one of America's leading theologians, Stanley Hauerwas. In this conversation stoked by the New Atheism debates, the two thinkers also discuss liberalism, the state of theology in the academy, and the ahistoricity of the field of history, and together they help to enrich the ongoing conversation about religion in modern life.

Stanley Hauerwas (SH): It is a delight to be in conversation with you again. To talk about your response to the New Atheism, it seems appropriate to start with your long-studied engagement with John Milton. In the last chapter of your book *How Milton Works*, you said that your response to liberalism, which I take it that the New Atheism nicely exhibits, is intimately tied to your understanding of how Milton works. I was quite taken by that, and I thought it might be interesting to hear you reflect on it.

Stanley Fish (SF): That's right, Stanley. My response to liberalism is not unlike many other people's responses to liberalism. I see it as an outgrowth of an atomization of the world, with freestanding, independent individuals tied to nothing and able to originate their own projects. That then leads to, in the legal field, the idea of personal rights as the center of the legal system and the idea that obligations and responsibilities are limited to those you enter into by contract. Therefore, all other kinds of obligations, like the obligation to be charitable or the obligation to be kind, are hard to fit into that system. Obviously a system like that is unable to take serious note of just the type of obligations most religions urge: not only loving your God, but loving your fellow creature as someone made in God's image. Therefore, the extreme discomfort that many liberals have with religious claims, that is, claims both in the sense of propositional claims and more importantly, claims on one's allegiance and attention.

A good example of this is John Rawls's book *Political Liberalism*. In both the first and the second edition he makes it clear that he is trying to respond to the challenge of making liberalism accommodate religion and to be fair to religion. But of course, that very vocabulary portrays the limitations and perhaps the shallowness of that hope, because what strong religiosity wants is not accommodation or fairness; strong religiosity wants strong allegiance. And that is something liberalism finds difficult to even contemplate.

SH: How do you think Milton's poetry works in a way to disabuse us of the liberal presumption that we are not situated?

SF: One of the ways that Milton's poetry disabuses us of that presumption is that the verse, although its technical and aesthetic virtuosity is undeniable, does not allow you or encourage you to rest in that virtuosity. At least in my reading of Milton, what is happening continually in one's experience of the poem is the demand to make distinctions, which are not only cognitive distinctions, but also moral distinctions, distinctions related to the objects of affection of the will itself. The poet is always encouraging you, for a moment at least, to be tempted in the wrong direction, and then he brings you up shortly in a way that is bracing and sometimes even unpleasant because it is a rebuke. That kind of experience demands that you reflect on the way you think about the most essential things in the world. It defeats the usual attempts of literature, or some kinds of literature, to distance itself from moral and religious commitments. Aestheticism is a part of the experience of reading Milton—it is almost a wonder that anyone could do these kinds of things with words—but aestheticism cannot be the large portion of one's response to Milton: he doesn't allow it.

SH: I was quite taken with your account of how Milton doesn't begin with human experience and then ask, "How do we make sense of God?" But his work instead suggests that you always begin with God, and then you say, "How do I make sense of my existence?"

SF: Right. That's the point of difference between Satan's account of his creation and Adam's account of his creation as Milton depicts them.[1]

SH: I often say that from a theological perspective, it is never a question of whether God exists but a question of whether we exist. I take it that Milton's poetry is an ongoing way of trying to help us understand the problematics of our existence and to see what it means to accept our existence as gift.

SF: Yes, and to help us accept our existence as creature. That is what Satan is incapable of doing, so he imagines, in effect, that he generated himself out of some primeval slime.

SH: How do you think those kinds of themes relate to a comment you picked up from Eagleton, which I assume has long been a part of your own work, namely that God is not an explanation?[2] Can you help us to think about what it means to deny that God is not an explanation?

1. See Milton, *Paradise Lost*.
2. See Eagleton, *Reason, Faith, and Revolution*.

SF: Yes, I think that Terry, who is both an old friend and an old antagonist, is very good on that point. The way that I usually put it, which is more theoretical, is that God is not an item in his own field. I sometimes chuckle when I hear the efforts of the kinds of atheists who demand a proof of God's existence, which is of course to get everything wrong from the beginning. And if you start there, without understanding what it means to conceive of or to accept or to acknowledge a God, then you are not going to get very far, and they do not get very far in their subsequent arguments. They think that they are refuting something, where in fact they haven't even taken seriously the existence and primacy of that which they think to refute even as a possibility. In a way, and I don't know if you would agree with this, I find their work profoundly uninteresting.

SH: [*Laughter.*] Of course, quite frankly I cannot bring myself to read most of it. One of my ways of putting it is that one of the problems of being a Christian today is that the secular has just become so stupid. They don't know how the grammar of our faith works. But I take it that that is partly our fault.

I want to read you a sentence from Eagleton. He says, "Yet it is most certainly Christianity itself which is primarily responsible for the intellectual sloppiness of its critics."[3] Do you have any comment on that?

SF: When Terry talks about that, he is usually attacking Catholicism. Also, it is part of his screed against the United States, which is also a theme of his book. He wants to find a place that the mindless materialism and faith in progress without content can be centrally located. The place he finds is the United States. I think that his singling out the kind of religious self-presentation that one associates with militiamen in Idaho or with some of the less palatable evangelical preachers is perhaps the weakest part of the book. He is blaming them for selling or retailing a brand of religion that is a discredit to the enterprise.

SH: I agree with that; although I'm more sympathetic with his criticisms of the state than you probably are, having still lingering Marxist sympathies myself.

SF: [*Laughter.*] Yes, I never had any Marxist sympathies.

3. Ibid., 55.

SH: [*Laughter.*] I know, I know. But I think that one of Eagleton's targets is also what might be called Protestant liberalism. For instance, you have leaders of Protestant churches who when asked, "What is your commitment to Jesus Christ?" say things like "I believe Jesus is our way to God, but then there are other ways to God." Now, when you have leaders of mainstream Protestant churches forgetting that Christians are Trinitarians—Jesus is not the way to God; Jesus is the Son of God—then it is not surprising that people who have little time for Christianity in general don't get it.

SF: And they are being told in such a way that they don't have to be bothered by it. If these "annoying people," whether they are called Christians or Jews or whatever, are really just saying that we are all on the same road—you've got your path, and I've got my path—then we can feel unthreatened by them and don't have to take their particular formulations very seriously, because it seems that in the end, they don't either.

SH: I think you would be very sympathetic with Terry's point that "the New Testament is a brutal destroyer of human illusions. If you follow Jesus and don't end up dead, it appears you have some explaining to do."[4]

SF: Yes, that is a great line. I wish I would have quoted it.

SH: It is a great line, and it is a line that is not very popular. It is hard to build church growth strategies based on a line like that. Of course, Christians today are deeply bothered by the fact that they are losing social and political power, and therefore, they want to show that they are on the side of a generalized humanism. This, I take it, is part of your problem and that you would not be for that strategy at all.

SF: No, I can certainly think of ways that an appeal to a generalized humanism might be useful, both politically and socially, but when you are trying to think through questions like the questions that are presented by Christianity and Judaism, a generalized humanism is not going to get you anywhere. It just so quickly becomes soft, and it is in effect a throwing up of the epistemological hands.

4. Ibid., 27.

SH: For those of us that are in the "field"—and to say that theology is a field is to express an oddity because we want it all—much of what you say sounds close to Karl Barth. Of course, Barth is often typed as the theologian that was against any kind of natural knowledge of a natural God. Do you have any sense of how your relationship with a theologian like that might work?

SF: No, I'm afraid not. Most of my engagements with these issues, as you yourself said earlier, have come from trying to wrestle with literary texts that are so obviously theological and often doctrinal. Milton is one case, and the Anglican poet George Herbert is an even purer case.

SH: There are, of course, deep disagreements between George Herbert and John Milton. Milton was anything but an orthodox Trinitarian.

SF: That's correct, and Milton was not, except at very few moments, operating in the Calvinist tradition, which Herbert certainly is.

SH: If you had to split the difference, who do you think makes the better case for Christian theology, Milton or Herbert?

SF: Herbert. It is no accident that Milton has been appropriated by different forms of humanistic projects throughout the years, most especially the project of the First Amendment in the United States or more generally the idea of freedom of expression that might appear anywhere in the world. Milton's *Areopagitica*, which is a plea for free expression, is taken up by humanists. A sentence from it is engraved in one of the walls of a room in the New York Public Library. Milton takes his place, at least in the free speech tradition, with people like John Stuart Mill, a noted enemy of religion, and Thomas Paine, another. And these people would never be persons who link themselves, or would be linked by others, with George Herbert.

SH: Let me read you a quote from David Bentley Hart, one of our most extraordinary stylists and thinkers today, from his newest book, *Atheist Delusions*: "Part of the enthralling promise of an age of reason was, at least at first, the prospect of a genuinely rational ethics, not bound to the local or tribal customs of this people or that, not limited to the moral precepts of any particular creed, but available to all reasoning minds regardless of culture and—when recognized—immediately compelling to the rational will. . . . If ever an age deserved to be thought an age of darkness, it is surely ours."[5] [*Laughter.*]

SF: [*Laughter.*] I always go back to a moment in Augustine, in I think the *De Trinitate*, where he explains quite succinctly that the laws of logical entailment work perfectly in a logical abstracted way but that those laws can't get started independent of some substantive proposition they do not contain. And that's it! So all this talk about simply harkening back to reason and having a rational, reasonable solution to all of life's vexing problems ceases to have any appeal at all.

SH: I'm very sympathetic, obviously, with going down the antifoundationalist road. I do wonder if it is a good idea, though, to say that every position finally depends on an act of faith. I think every position depends on what R. G. Collingwood would call an absolute presupposition.[6] But I don't want to call it faith, because for me, faith is faithfully following Christ. So the word *faith* becomes a bit too loose for me.

SF: I understand your unease with the word. In polemics, as you know, one is often put in a position where it becomes at least useful to stretch the limits of a word further than they should perhaps be stretched. So when so many of the atheists argue for reason or empirical facts and against what they conceive to be faith, it becomes a strategy that I use to import faith into their worlds where they don't think it properly belongs. It becomes a move in a game that—and this is what I think you are suggesting—may have costs that we don't want to pay.

SH: At least it does for me as a theologian.

SF: I can see that. Of course, I am not a theologian—although I love theology and love to think about theology. The responders to the pieces that I've written on these matters, especially in the *New York Times*, always want me to come out and say where I myself stand religiously or where I

---

5. Hart, *Atheist Delusions*, 106.
6. See Collingwood, *Essay on Metaphysics*.

stand in terms of religion. That is something I have never done, will never do, and will not do here!

SH: Of course [*laughter*], it never occurred to me to ask you. How would you know where you stand?

SF: That's true, too. Although I don't think I can take refuge in that generalization. One of the things that I do when I write columns for the *New York Times*—and I periodically have to explain this to exasperated readers—is look at the way arguments work, or more likely, look at the way some arguments don't work. And that is the way I operate when I talk about the atheists. I am both amused and to some extent appalled by the total flimsiness of their arguments. That is what I write about. Of course, the explanation doesn't take, perhaps because the roster of exasperated readers is continually changing.

SH: I often say that I can't stand Kant or "Can't," and I assume that goes some way to explaining why you go after Christopher Hitchens so much.

SF: That is almost personal. I met him once. We were at a panel together in Hartford at the Mark Twain House. I don't remember the subject, and I don't even remember if he was sober, which would have been an unlikely occasion, but he was certainly Christopher Hitchens as evidenced by his rambling on and on.

At that time, he had just finished his book attacking Mother Teresa, and he was complaining in a way that was a boast that no American publisher would ever take a book like that. I let him go on for a while, and then I stood up and said, "I happen to be an American publisher, I am the director of the Duke University Press, and I shall be happy to accept your book!"

SH: No, you haven't told me this story. What did he say?

SF: He shut up, but only briefly!

SH: I see [*laughter*], so partly you were directing your attention toward him because of a strong personal relationship.

SF: Well, it was very brief, but I had an intense dislike of him as an example of the kind of person that used to fill English departments: supercilious Brits, usually drunk, extremely well educated in the sense that they had read a lot of things but were incapable of understanding any of them.

SH: How do you account for that?

SF: I don't know. There are certainly exceptions, like my friend David Lodge, but Christopher Hitchens is just the quintessential type.

SH: How much do you think the "Hitchens-like" phenomenon tells us something about the mis-education of the modern university?

SF: I think that to some extent it tells us something about the way in which many subjects, including law, are taught as if they didn't have a history. Therefore, there is no knowledge in many disciplines that the questions the discipline is now worrying about have been in the purview of theological inquiry for many hundreds of years, and often these questions have been addressed in ways that are infinitely more sophisticated than the ways of a truncated modern look.

SH: I went to ask Seymour Mauskopf in the Duke history department who taught their methodology course, and he said, "We don't have one."
    So I asked, "Who teaches the history of history?"
    And he said again that they don't have one. I thought, "What? How could that be that they don't teach the history of history?" I understand now that they are going to start doing that, but it is interesting that history as a discipline seems to have gotten away with less self-consciousness than any discipline in the modern university.

SF: Yes, well as you no doubt know, history was among the fields in the humanities and social sciences that was most resistant to the turn to theory, which in most disciplines occurred in the late 1950s to mid 1960s. There were a few like Hayden White who tried to import theoretical notions into history, but he and others were resisted. And what the turn to theory meant for disciplines—and this is ironic—is that disciplines suddenly became aware of their own historicity, of the way in which the routines that they ran with a certain degree of confidence and the questions that they asked and considered obligatory had an origin in debates and controversies that could at any moment be revived again. That kind of knowledge really did change many of the ways work was done in literature, anthropology, sociology, and other disciplines. Historians, however, were impervious.

SH: It is very interesting to ask why. It makes you think that history has such an ideological function for reinforcing the presumption that the way things happened is the way that things had to happen that they just can't break out of any other alternative.

SF: And it's also a part of an explanation of the popularity of history, or at least popular history. The books of the kind written by Michael Beschloss or Doris Kearns Goodwin or the serial liar Joseph Ellis—their work is devoured by the middlebrow, *New York Review of Books* public, and these people are always on television and presented as wise. It is the kind of knowledge, or the way of thinking about knowledge, that is very reassuring to people who don't want their forms of thought disturbed in any way.

SH: And if you are a theologian in today's university, that makes it a pretty difficult place to be.

SF: Well, if I may ask, what is the state of theology in the universities these days?

SH: I think the answer is that theology does not exist. Theology could not become a discipline within the undergraduate curriculum in any major university, and liberal arts colleges tend to copy what goes on in major research universities. Theology didn't know how to present the grammar of faith in a way that wouldn't appear to be belying the democratic sensibilities of the students, that is, that everything has to be presented fairly. So I think theology doesn't exist in the modern university. This, I think, helps explain why secular critics simply have never confronted what a serious theological argument would look like.

SF: I think that's right; although, as you know, I did inaugurate a chair in Catholic studies at the University of Illinois in Chicago.

SH: I think that part of our pathos today is that after theology was run out of the undergraduate curriculums, we simply had no place that people would be at least even minimally introduced to the complexity of the Christian or Jewish faith. We are paying heavy prices for that.

SF: I see that again in the responses to my columns in the *New York Times*. Of course, *New York Times* readers are very predictable, but a huge percentage of them reject religion because it doesn't have a ready answer to what they take to be the problems of life. When you try to tell them that in fact religion is going to tell you the problems of life are not quite what you have always assumed them to be but are much more difficult and much deeper, it is not something they can even hear.

SH: I think that's right. What can you do when you have to tell people that they have a bourgeois soul and they are fundamentally superficial? Where are you going to go? The *ad hominem* unfortunately works too often times.

I often say that if you want to know where people's faith is articulated today, it is in medical schools. That is where people are trained to serve people who think that if you get good enough medicine you have the possibility of getting out of life alive. And that is the reason why places like Duke North and Duke South now look like cathedrals. Duke Chapel is just an anomaly; no one knows what to make of it—that it is just there to declare the glory of God.

SF: Speaking to the role of theology in the academy, I do want to say that I find that my most satisfying pedagogical experience is teaching the religion course on the First Amendment. Before my students begin to read one of the cases, I try to introduce them to the religious issues and to understand what a religious claim is, which I find they mostly don't understand. So it is wonderful to be able to teach a doctrinal subject in the law school sense of doctrinal and to introduce students to doctrine and even to dogma, a word they always misunderstand. This is a double pleasure, which I very much cherish.

SH: I take that one of your strongest points, which you have made again and again, is that nothing the critics might raise hasn't been raised internal to Christian and Jewish thought from the beginning.

SF: Not only that it has already been raised, but that it is largely the content of that thought.

SH: Right, for example, I always point out to people when they raise questions of suffering, "Have you read the Psalms lately? You know, I've been faithful; you've beaten the hell out of me, God, but you are still God." I take it that that logic is unassailable.

SF: Yes, and I think that Terry Eagleton is very good on that point.

SH: Exactly. Well, it is an honor to talk to you again, thank you.

SF: Thank you.

14

The New Atheism and the Spiritual Landscape of the West: An Interview with Charles Taylor

RONALD A. KUIPERS

The Other Journal (TOJ): I want to ask you about your thoughts on atheism in general and explore what you have to say about atheism at the end of your new book, *A Secular Age*.[1] I'm referring in particular to what you say on pages 768–69, where you describe two possible futures for the development of religion in the West. The first future flows out of mainline secularization theory, which predicts the continuous erosion of the public relevance of religious traditions. The second future, however, foresees religious traditions remaining an important aspect of people's ongoing spiritual search for meaning.

Charles Taylor (CT): My money is on future number two, that is, the second of the two alternatives I outline in my book. I don't really think that religion is going to fade away and that religiously defined alternatives will be less and less common. On the contrary—well, I don't know if you've read the whole book, given that it's so darn long [*laughter*].

TOJ: I've read it twice, actually, and taught a thirteen-week graduate seminar where we worked through the entire book quite closely [*laughter*].

CT: Wonderful, there is at least somebody then [*laughter*]. As I was saying, in my final chapter, I suggest that future number two is much more likely, and I hope that the previous chapters will have prepared the reader

1. Taylor, *Secular Age*.

to see why I believe that religious alternatives will proliferate rather than fade away.

We are going to have something like the pattern that I was just describing, which is not only a pattern of great variation and constant innovation, but also a pattern of different views between the generations. I mean, it is not uncommon now for children to break from the religious views of their parents. As a matter of fact, this is the case in many Western societies, independent of whether there are very high rates of religious belief and practice, like in the United States, or very low levels, as in countries like Sweden. For example, in the United States there is a recent Pew report suggesting that one in three people have changed their religious affiliation in the course of their lives. Now, this may be something that is relatively trivial, because Americans have a great variety of denominations, and you can move from this denomination to that denomination without there being any kind of great transition or conversion. Nevertheless, it does indeed say something about the nature and future of Western societies.

TOJ: Could you elaborate further on this second future? You seem to suggest that this future is one in which human beings continue to struggle with religious questions, and more broadly, with the deep sense of the basic religiousness of life.

CT: That's how I would describe it, and the thing is that we really don't have a generally accepted language or term to describe what this is. I think I would call it a sense of, say, *eternity*, but I know that there are people on the other side of my tradition who would react negatively to that term.

TOJ: So you have tried the word *fullness* as a word that might be more universally accepted.

CT: Yes, I've used this as a generic term because I think everybody has some sense of, and desire for, a fantastically realized life, a life realized to the full. But in talking with people and reading reviews of the book, I've found that I'm often totally misunderstood on this. They thought that fullness could only be applied to explicitly religious positions, while the whole point was that I was looking for a generic term that applied to all people, whether religious or nonreligious. But fullness made people shudder, which might show that the search for a universally acceptable term might be mission impossible.

TOJ: Maybe that happens because you talk about fullness as something very generic that everyone can relate to, but then you proceed to offer your unique take on fullness as something that involves a sense of transcendence. So there are secularists, atheists, or nonreligious people who might not have a problem with the language of fullness per se, but who are strongly opposed to a notion of fullness that leans on the language of transcendence. It seems that it is transcendence with which they really have a problem.

CT: Well, what I tried to do in the book, and again it is so hard that it may be mission impossible, is to lay out a picture of the scene in which we are all involved, a scene that people could agree on even if they are coming from different positions. But I also wanted to add that I think we should also have full disclosure, that is, communicating where I am coming from, where I am situating myself in the scene, and how I would then read the scene from that position. So while I do think we can come to a general agreement on the scene—the scene I just described a minute ago that's characterized by spiritual fragmentation and proliferation—I don't expect my readers to all agree with my more particular reading of the scene.

I think everyone who is really open and honest will acknowledge that this is our scene, or our common situation, and that it has these three features that I outline in my book: great variety, great movement, and a great potential to be deeply shaken by other positions. I think everyone could agree to that; I think everyone should agree to that. This is a description in which I am very well invested, but of course this scene is lived from different positions. And I think that in a book like this, one should do a variety of things, both describing general features that all can agree to and being open and honest about one's own unique position, what I describe as full disclosure, or disclosing one's particular way of looking at things. Sadly, however, my attempt at full disclosure at the end of the book seems to have polluted the entire book for some people.

TOJ: I really want to talk more about this idea of full disclosure. It seems like as soon as you do something like that as a religious philosopher, the academy immediately assumes you're doing theology rather than philosophy and that you've gone too particularistic and are no longer talking universally.

CT: Or they think you are trying to pull one over on them.

TOJ: Right, yes, something like that. I mean I think that in the Immanent Frame blog, Jonathan Sheehan did quite a good job of appreciating your book, but even he comes to a point where he says that "by the time the reader reaches chapter twenty it becomes clear that the book is an explicit brief for a theological critique of secularism."[2] It appears that he also felt like you turned from philosophical description to theological confession, and in that way, you really were trying to pull one over on him. Sheehan's critique is operating on a certain assumption, and I am curious to hear what you think about this widely held assumption, according to which secular philosophers consider themselves not to operate with the same type of "fiduciary" spin that religious philosophers do.

CT: I think that people who react like Sheehan have a huge a priori assumption operating. I've actually written on this in the Immanent Frame very recently, but I've been working on this issue with Habermas and others for years.[3] That is, they have what is to me this weird idea that there is such a thing as reason alone, or bare reason. In other words, they assume that there are two kinds of people, those who operate on the grounds of secular reason, who reason with reason alone, and those who operate on the grounds of religious reason, who reason from extra premises derived from revelation that are uncontrolled rationally.

So when you admit you have religious faith, you immediately get scrutinized to make sure you're not slipping in stuff. And I suppose that in my book it looks for a long time as if I'm not slipping in stuff, but then I do this full-disclosure thing at the end that makes them suspicious.

TOJ: But this is strange because it's no secret that you're a religious person.

CT: I know.

2. Sheehan, "Framing the Middle."
3. Taylor, "Secularism and Critique."

TOJ: If I can speculate, I guess what is maybe a little disarming is that, while your views are present in your previous writings, in *A Secular Age* you really come out much more strongly in terms of a thick description of your worldview.

CT: Yeah, that blows their minds. I should have told them not to read chapter twenty [*laughter*]. Or maybe I shouldn't have put chapter twenty in the book, but I do think it really is something you ought to do. I mean the subject matter lends itself to this kind of disclosure because all throughout the book I am describing positions other than my own, so at some point it's proper to disclose where I am in the scene I've been describing.

TOJ: Would it be fair to say that you're describing in a general, and therefore in a broadly acceptable way, the history of religious development and the development of secularization in the West?

CT: That's right—

TOJ: And one of the conclusions you come to is that what you have is this incredible proliferation or fragmentation of spiritual options or orientations, and then in chapter twenty you say, "OK, now this is the one I inhabit." You are switching registers here, are you not?

CT: Yes, I am definitely switching registers. But I spent a lot of time in the book describing phenomenologically what it was like to move away from Christianity, to reject Christianity, really, and to be excited by Deism, by Jacobinism, by Nietzsche, and then more recently by George Bataille, by Robinson Jeffers, and others. So why wouldn't I describe what it's like to convert out of this view as well and into Christianity, which is really what chapter twenty is all about? What I want to describe is a certain form of life shared by various people, people who begin stuck in a closed reading of what in the book I call "the immanent frame," but who then break out of this closed reading. Take someone like Charles Péguy, who was originally an unbelieving socialist but ended his life a practicing Roman Catholic, and someone like Flannery O'Connor, who articulates the experience of beginning to see this other dimension of existence, or Gerard

Manley Hopkins, who moves through the poetics of post-Romanticism and then into Christian faith. All these people are people who have been in this kind of boundary situation, which is where I identify myself. This is simply another kind of experience, and there is no reason why this shouldn't also be part of the phenomenological description in the book, except that full disclosure requires me to say, "These are all very interesting positions, but I am here."

TOJ: That reminds me of Jeffrey Stout's *Democracy and Tradition.*[4] One of Stout's main arguments in that book is that we really want full disclosure of people's religious positions in these kinds of public conversations, because what we want is to be able to have "abnormal" conversations, conversations between people inhabiting radically different perspectives, and as long as we keep needing to check these differences at the door, so to speak, then we'll never actually get to talking about what it is we really need to talk about. So I guess I'm just affirming the legitimacy of providing full disclosure, even within a book that is predominantly philosophical; at least, I hope that such disclosure wouldn't make the book nonphilosophical, anyway. Do you have an opinion on the relationship between faith and philosophy, or on the assumption that, when you switch a register and provide full disclosure, all of a sudden, you're not doing philosophy anymore, but you're doing theology?

CT: I think that last conclusion is totally unfounded. What you need to do is to be aware of where your interlocutors are standing and be able to distinguish between things that it ought to be possible to come to agreement on; it's important, if we are to go on living our lives together, that we are aware that the fact that we disagree on these fundamental issues does not mean that we need to be total enemies. And my book is really an exercise in this, in that it paints a picture of the condition of the world we are living in, and in a way, it is a picture that I think I can get people to agree on. And I have persuaded some people to agree on it, even though they are coming from an entirely different position.

TOJ: Right, I think a lot of what your book does is a sort of immanent critique, in that when you come to discuss the views you don't hold, you still try to describe how things might look from those perspectives, including

4. Stout, *Democracy and Tradition.*

what is actually attractive about them. And I think the service you're doing by including chapter twenty is saying something like, "From within the view I actually inhabit, this is what I find attractive about it." And it's not some kind of logically airtight argument, but rather a rhetorical move to say, "This is why it persuades me, and I leave it to you to determine whether you find it a persuasive picture or not."

CT: Exactly, exactly.

TOJ: Just to bring us back to the topic of atheism, I wonder if you have any opinion regarding those who are being called the "New Atheists," say Christopher Hitchens, Richard Dawkins, and Sam Harris, who happen to be quite militant in their rhetoric.

CT: Yes, I happen to have quite a negative view of these folks. I think their work is very intellectually shoddy. There are two things that perhaps I am just totally allergic to. The first is that they all believe that there really are some knockdown arguments against belief in God. And of course, this is something you can only believe if you have a scientistic, reductionist conception and explanation of everything in the world, including human beings. If you do have such a view that everything is to be explained in terms of physics and the movement of atoms and the like, then certain forms of access to God are just closed. For example, there are certain human experiences that might direct us to God, but these would all be illusory if everything could be explained in scientific terms. I spend a lot of time reflecting and writing on the various human sciences and how they can be tempted into a kind of reductionism, and not only would I say that the jury is out on that, but I would argue that the likelihood of that turning out to be the proper understanding of human beings is very small. And the problem is that they just assume this reductionistic view.

The second thing I am allergic to is that they keep going on and on about the relationship between religion and violence, which on one level is fine because there is a lot of religiously caused violence. But what they consistently fail to acknowledge is that the twentieth century was full of various atheists who were rampaging around killing millions of people. Thus, it is simply absurd that at the end of the twentieth century someone would continue to advance the thesis that religion is the main cause of violence. You'd think these people were writing in 1750, and that would be quite understandable if you were Voltaire or Locke, but to say this in 2008, well, it just takes my breath away.

But then what we need to do, and this is something many religious people fail to do, is to consider why this phenomenon of the New Atheism is happening at this time. Atheists are reacting in the same way that religious fundamentalists reacted in the past. They are people who have been very comfortable with a sense that their particular position is what makes sense of everything and so on, and then when they are confronted by something else they just go bananas and throw up the most incredibly bad arguments in a tone of indignation and anger. And that's the problem with the master narrative of secularization, what's called the secularization thesis—you know, the idea that religion is a thing of the past, that it's disappearing, that it did all these terrible things, but it's going to go away and so on. People got lulled into it and when religion comes back, they are just undone.

TOJ: Or when they realize it never went away—

CT: Right, not only did they not notice that it was always there and never really went away, but phenomenologically in their experience it came back suddenly. Religion returned! And why? Well, for no apparent reason. It doesn't make any sense in light of the secularization thesis. And it's wrecking the whole universe they had tidily built. So they get terribly angry. And that makes for a very curious kind of atheism. So this tells us something about the zeitgeist, about what's happening, about how people have bought very deeply into a particular master narrative, namely the secularization thesis that religion is on its way out, from which they are getting a certain degree of spiritual comfort, and now that this has been disrupted, they are reacting with rage.

TOJ: That's very interesting. So if I'm hearing you correctly, you're saying that the extreme atheistic reaction to the return of religion is actually a spiritual reaction to an interrupted spiritual narrative.

CT: Exactly, and people are very deeply invested in this narrative—we're all deeply invested in our spiritual narratives, but we don't all have this sense that history is on our side. It's terrible in that sense.

TOJ: In *A Secular Age,* you suggest that there is a parallel between these militant atheists and dogmatic religious people. Would it be on that score?

CT: Exactly, exactly. The militancy is stronger in the United States than in Canada because there is this sense among many American Christians, more so among Protestants than Catholics, that America is founded on a certain kind of interdenominational Protestant Christianity. I mean we know that a lot of these founders were closet Deists, like Thomas Jefferson, but for the majority of Americans it really was about a providential carrying out of God's plan and so on. And America is now split between people who hold onto this kind of national identity and others, a much smaller but more influential group who dominate the media and the universities and so on, that have a completely different read on America's founding. The same Constitution and the same constitutional rules are read in a secularist light; that is, there is no privileged position and that all religions are equally to be abstracted from. And the upshot is that each of these groups thinks that the other has betrayed America and is being un-American.

TOJ: So would you see both the religious fundamentalists and the militant atheists as reactionaries? As people who drive wedges between people and lead to more misunderstanding and demonization?

CT: Absolutely.

15

Worshipping a Flying Teapot?
What To Do When Christianity Looks Ridiculous

RANDAL RAUSER

Today, many Christian theologians treat arguments for the faith as passé, as an embarrassing vestige of modernity.

Take, for instance, Robert Webber's book *The Younger Evangelicals*. According to Webber, the clash of apologetic arguments is not nearly as helpful in witnessing to the faith and furthering mutual understanding as the exchange of personal stories and living lives of integrity. As Webber puts it, "In a pagan world where every person 'lives for himself,' the pagans don't cry, 'Look at the power of their rational arguments' but 'see how they love one another!'"[1]

Based on these assumptions, Webber adopted a rather unorthodox approach when he was invited to engage in a public debate with an atheist. He recounts:

> In order to shift the discussion away from arguments for or against God's existence, I used my opening comments to inform my opponent and the listening audience that I would not discuss traditional arguments for the existence of God. When asked, "Well, how then shall we proceed?" I answered, "Let's talk about the reality of the communities of Israel and Jesus. Let's probe those stories to uncover what they tell us about the origin, meaning, and destiny of

1. Webber, *Younger Evangelicals*, 95. Similarly Dave Tomlinson writes: "Part of the rub with post-evangelicals is that most evangelicals rely on apologetics to explain their faith. But apologetics can't satisfy the postmodern appetite for mystery, paradox, and imagination. People are desperate for myth, art, and story" (*Post Evangelical*, 83).

the world." In this way I shifted the discussion from propositions based on evidence to stories based on faith.[2]

I sympathize with Webber's approach—many people who come to these types of debates are fiercely angry at Christians and expect to encounter an intolerant, red-faced Christian fundamentalist who will vindicate their prejudices. In that context, the sharper and more ruthless the debater, the more the audience is likely to be alienated and vindicated. Perhaps with that kind of prejudice operative, an individual humbly sharing his story might indeed represent a more effective Christian witness.

At the same time, we must recognize the serious tradeoff entailed by Webber's approach insofar as it refuses to address any of the legitimate intellectual objections people have to belief. And with these obstacles not even being acknowledged, it is doubtful that people will be able to hear his story. By comparison, if a Mormon missionary comes to my door, I don't want to hear about the burning in his bosom until I have heard him address the historical and philosophical problems with Mormonism.

Webber's refusal to acknowledge that people have real intellectual obstacles to belief reminds me of the man who responded to a skeptic's challenge of the historicity of the resurrection by biting into an apple and asking: "Does this apple taste sweet or sour?" The skeptic replied that he had no idea because he had not tasted the apple, to which the man replied: "Neither have you tasted my Jesus." Is that *really* all that we are obliged to say to the skeptic?

The case of Antony Flew, one of the world's leading academic atheists of the second half of the twentieth century, illustrates the continuing value of rational argumentation. In 2003 Flew "came out of the closet" to confess his conversion to theism (though not yet any particular religion). Although many atheists were quick to dismiss Flew's conversion as that of an old man confronting his mortality, Flew explained that his conversion was forced by the cumulative intellectual weight of various philosophical and theological arguments.[3]

While it is clear that argument remains important in "contending for the faith," Webber is correct that people bring a lot more to debates than seminar room quandaries. Some years ago, when I was living in London, I

2. Webber, *Younger Evangelicals*, 83.

3. See Flew and Habermas, "My Pilgrimage from Atheism to Theism"; cf. Flew, *There Is a God*.

attended a debate on the existence of God at the local academic bookshop. As I entered the room, I was greeted by a young smiling representative of the British Humanist Association (BHA) who welcomed me warmly (in the style of Campus Crusade for Christ) and handed me some BHA literature. Over the next couple of hours, I was deeply impacted not by the arguments for or against theism, but rather by the clearly antireligious atmosphere of the room.

The atheist debater (Nigel Warburton) was a witty fellow who had the audience in his pocket as he made disparaging comments about God and religion. Indeed, I was taken aback by the deep level of hostility and derision toward Christianity, and theism generally, within the audience. I left that evening with a new appreciation for the depth of unbelief and how much more than a skilled theistic debater would be required to get Christianity a serious hearing. Many of the audience members may as well have been attending a debate over the existence of Santa Claus. No matter how clever the pro-Santa debater would have been, he would not have increased the plausibility of his hypothesis among the audience one iota, for they had written off the fat man long ago.

If Antony Flew's conversion illustrates the continuing need for rational argument, the rise of the so-called New Atheism illustrates the deeper problem with the basic plausibility of Christianity. The leaders of the New Atheism, writers like Sam Harris, Christopher Hitchens, Daniel Dennett, and Richard Dawkins, have all written bestsellers repudiating Christianity, religion, and theism.[4] What is interesting is that the New Atheists appear unaware of the revolution in Christian philosophy of religion over the last forty years.[5] To be frank, the sophistication of their respective critiques is closer to the level of the crude village atheist or the curmudgeonly troll who emerges from under his bridge to throw stones at passing parishioners. The New Atheism is notable not for the power of its argumentation, but rather for the heightened intensity of its rhetoric.

What we learn from this growing list of bestsellers is that the New Atheists assume that religious commitment is tantamount to belief in a "celestial teapot" or "flying spaghetti monster." The teapot analogy,

---

4. See for instance Harris, *Letter to a Christian Nation*; Hitchens, *God Is Not Great*; Dennett, *Breaking the Spell*; Dawkins, *God Delusion*.

5. But academic atheists, particularly those concerned with naturalism and atheism, certainly are aware of advances in Christian philosophy of religion, and they are troubled by it. See Q. Smith, "Metaphilosophy of Naturalism."

suggested originally by Bertrand Russell, was taken up with some relish by Dawkins: "To borrow a point from Bertrand Russell, we must be equally agnostic about the theory that there is a china teapot in elliptical orbit around the Sun. We can't disprove it. But that doesn't mean the theory that there is a teapot is on level terms with the theory that there isn't."[6] In 2005, Bobby Henderson updated Russell's analogy by inventing the "flying spaghetti monster" along with a parody religion that worships the "spaghedeity."[7]

While Christian philosophers could deftly dispense with this trite comparison by pointing out disanalogies between God and these fantastical posits of the atheologian,[8] there is a trap lying in the bushes of the classic "damned if you do; damned if you don't" variety. In short, the Christian apologist finds herself in a sort of quicksand of implausibility such that the more she lashes out in defense, the quicker she sinks. The situation is put well by Sam Harris:

> Atheism is not a philosophy; it is not even a view of the world; it is simply an admission of the obvious. In fact, "atheism" is a term that should not even exist. No one ever needs to identify himself as a "non-astrologer" or a "non-alchemist." We do not have words for people who doubt that Elvis is still alive or that aliens have traversed the galaxy only to molest ranchers and their cattle. Atheism is nothing more than the noises reasonable people make in the presence of unjustified religious beliefs.[9]

It hardly matters if what Harris says is erroneous, for he adeptly captures a widespread sentiment that theism is now widely considered guilty until proven innocent while the very attempt to prove it innocent appears to undermine one's credibility!

This dilemma brings me to the heart of my thesis: restoring Christianity's place as a live intellectual option requires not simply superior rational argumentation, but the restoration of a background framework in which Christian claims seem minimally plausible. As such, we should think of this project with both the long-term and short-term in

6. Dawkins, *Devil's Chaplain*, 149; cf. Dawkins, *God Delusion*, 74–75.

7. The parody religion has grown enormously popular. See the official Web site of the "church" at http://www.venganza.org/.

8. See, for instance, Plantinga's discussion of "'The Great Pumpkin Objection' to theistic belief in "Reason and Belief in God."

9. Harris, *Letter to a Christian Nation*, 51.

view. In the long-term, we should seek a deepened Christian contribution to culture with the understanding that this will produce the by-product of restoring the background plausibility of Christianity. And within the short-term, we should argue for the faith in a way that applies arguments with a consideration of their background plausibility within specific contexts. With this project in mind, I will first provide an expanded account of how the current implausibility of theism marginalizes rational defenses of belief, before developing an overview of what is required in the long- and short-term to restore the plausibility of theism generally and Christianity specifically.

God and the Flying Spaghetti Monster

Unfortunately, in their debates, the New Atheists frequently raise the logical problem of evil without demonstrating any awareness of the commonly cited free will defense.[10] According to Alvin Plantinga, perhaps the philosopher most closely associated with the free will defense, it may be that in any possible world where God creates free creatures at least some of those creatures choose to sin, and thus there is no logical contradiction between God being perfectly good and omnipotent and evil existing.[11]

But while Plantinga's argument explains the existence of moral evil, it does not explain the existence of natural evil, that is, evil which arises from the natural world (e.g., earthquakes and tsunamis). Plantinga thus sought to explain the origin of natural evil by reducing it to moral evil: namely, the evil actions of demonic beings.[12] While the proposal was offered to address a specific logical problem, Plantinga's proposal earned him a place in Daniel Dennett's facetious *Philosophical Lexicon* (a book of pseudo-technical terms that are humorous wordplays off the names of famous philosophers). In the Plantinga entry, the verb "alvinize" was defined by Dennett as follows: "To stimulate protracted discussion by making a bizarre claim, [as in,] 'His contention that natural evil is due to

10. For instance, ibid., 55.

11. See Plantinga, *God, Freedom, and Evil*. Although Plantinga's work was significant, it does not address either the inductive problem of evil (that is, the problem that God's existence seems unlikely given the amount and distribution of evil) or the pastoral problem of evil (how one can believe in/trust God in light of the personal experience of evil).

12. Ibid., 58.

Satanic agency alvinized his listeners."[13] This example illustrates the fact that logically valid arguments for theism do not necessarily increase the perceived plausibility of Christian belief.

A plausible religious system is, to use William James's terminology, a live option for belief, one that, even if we do not accept it, we still take seriously and do not immediately consider it ridiculous. By contrast, a credible religious system is one that we consider to have requisite rationality, evidential support, and internal coherence. Christian apologists have often focused on establishing the narrow credibility of Christianity, without due concern for its background plausibility. Such is arguably the case when Plantinga explains natural evil by invoking demons: though he may have won a logical battle, the overall war for Christian plausibility is lost, or at least severely hampered. That is, while his argument might remove one more logical impediment to Christianity, it also makes it look more ridiculous than ever.

In *The Gravedigger File*, Os Guinness makes the point that Christianity could be undermined at this level of basic plausibility. As Guinness observes, "Roman Catholicism is more likely to *seem* true in Eire than in Egypt, just as Mormonism is in Salt Lake City than in Singapore, and Marxism in Moscow than in Mecca. In each case, plausibility comes from a world of shared support."[14] Thus, once the emerging consensus among elite and popular culture views Christianity as ridiculous, it becomes that much more difficult to sustain belief and make a compelling case for Christian faith. C. S. Lewis recognized the significance of this shift as he commented on the difficulty of defending the Apostles' Creed in a world that dismissed biblical cosmology as absurd:

> When once a man is convinced that Christianity *in general* implies a local "Heaven," a flat earth, and a God who can have children, he naturally listens with impatience to our solutions of particular difficulties and our defenses against particular objections. The more ingenious we are in such solutions and defenses the more perverse we seem to him.[15]

In this reference to the perversity of a defense, one might well have been talking of Plantinga's invocation of demons creating earthquakes. As a

13. Dennett and Steglich-Petersen, *Philosophical Lexicon*.
14. Guinness, *Gravedigger File*, 36, 35.
15. Lewis, *Miracles*, 109. Italics in original.

result, even as Christian philosophers and theologians develop logically tight defenses of the faith, the whole enterprise begins to appear increasingly *ridiculous,* with belief in God being compared to belief in flying spaghetti monsters and celestial teapots.[16]

The Long View: Arguments and Christian Cultural Renewal

If, as Guinness and Lewis suggest, plausibility comes from a world of shared support, then we should work at constructing that world. But perhaps we might begin by identifying some of the nonrational factors that make Christianity look ridiculous. Here is a smattering of examples from a North American context:

1. Church roadside signs with trite captions like "This church is prayer-conditioned"

2. Pedophile priests and white-suited televangelists with impeccable hair

3. "Christian" bumper stickers with captions like "My boss is a Jewish carpenter" and "I believe in the Big Bang. God said 'Bang!' and it happened"

4. Low tithing rates and a disinterest in social justice

5. The unabashed marketing of the gospel as a consumer item and the reduction of pastors to life coaches who offer motivational speeches

6. Attempts to get creation science (or Intelligent Design) into the public school system through litigation

7. Blind nationalism and the identification of Christianity with one political party

8. Insipid, limp-wristed examples of Christian kitsch from Thomas Kinkade to Bible action figures

Factors such as these conspire to make Christians look comical, dangerous, innocuous, irrelevant, and generally unpleasant. As a result, they serve to marginalize the Christian voice as irrelevant and make it much

16. Guinness observes, "If secularization provides inviting snow conditions and tempts people to buy a new ski outfit, it makes religious beliefs seem as unseasonal as swimwear in a blizzard" (*Gravedigger File,* 57).

easier to project the same absurdity and irrelevancy upon the deity that Christians worship.[17]

Of course, more is required than merely rooting out the most embarrassing products of Christian culture. In addition to eliminating kitsch culture, anti-intellectualism, and the un-Christlikeness that undermines the plausibility of the faith, one must also seek to build the plausibility of the faith, and one strategic effort toward this end is the formation of Christians who are leading contributions to the broader culture, rather than sub-par members of the Christian ghetto. In this regard, few have equaled the clear vision of Pope Nicholas V, who outlined a specific program to transform Rome from a backwater collection of medieval villages to the cultural center of Europe:

> [In order] to create solid and stable convictions in the minds of the uncultured masses, there must be something that appeals to the eye: a popular faith, sustained only on doctrines, will never be anything but feeble and vacillating. But if the authority of the Holy See were visibly displayed in majestic buildings, imperishable memorials and witnesses seemingly planted by the hand of God himself, belief would grow and strengthen like a tradition from one generation to another, and all the world would accept and revere it.[18]

While our context, aim, and means all differ radically from that of Renaissance Rome,[19] we can find insight in Nicholas's proposal. Western culture needs Christianity as a revitalized cultural force, both for the intrinsic benefits that this would bring, as well as for the proximate goal of restoring Christian plausibility. Nicholas was exactly right that belief is fostered from within a cultural context, though he was wrong to think this is limited to the "uncultured masses"; indeed, a world of shared support would increase Christian plausibility among intellectuals as well.

So what might this look like in today's terms? Here we can briefly consider two areas: music and architecture. Throughout history, Christians have witnessed to their faith through innovative and inspiring music, from Handel's "Messiah" to John Coltrane's "A Love Supreme"

17. One can only speculate to what extent these types of factors prevent Antony Flew from moving beyond a minimal deism to a Christian faith.

18. Cited in Duffy, *Saints and Sinners*, 139.

19. And need it be said that we should hardly wish to emulate the renaissance popes in our pursuit of this goal?

and more recently the eclectic offerings of indie rocker Sufjan Stevens. Unfortunately, these days much of the more challenging work is drowned out by the nauseating and banal offerings of the CCM mainstream.

A similar problem is evident with church architecture. Consider Burton Cummings's song "I'm Scared," in which Cummings describes his experience of walking into a cathedral in New York and being overcome by a transcendent presence of otherness.[20] It is not that one could not have a mystical experience upon walking into a contemporary pastel, theatre-style sanctuary replete with ferns and dove-emblazoned banners—it's just that it seems so unlikely.

Intuitively we know that while churches built today are marvelously functional, they are also typically devoid of character or religious sensibility, let alone transcendence. Just how far we have fallen is evident when we consider the Sagrada Familia Church, the magnificent vision of that mad genius Gaudi, which has been under construction for the last one hundred years. When it is finally completed (which, with current estimates, could be as early as 2026) its eighteen massive towers, including the 170-meter tower of Jesus Christ, will dominate Barcelona.

Each time a Christian contributes positively to culture, he or she is unwittingly expanding the space of the Christian universe, and brick by brick reconstructing the vibrancy, and so plausibility, of the Christian worldview. We can expect that the building of a formidable Christian culture to match the glories of antiquity will, like the Sagrada Familia, take decades to construct. But as Christian politicians, artists, community planners, musicians, architects, and the rest all contribute to the reformation of Western society, they are indirectly contributing to the plausibility of the Christian worldview itself, and thus making the efforts of the Christian apologist that much more likely to find success.[21] And if someone were to object that this is too idealistic and that our world needs evangelists and social workers, not cultural and intellectual ambassadors,

---

20. Although Cummings has described this church in concert as the "Cathedral of St. Thomas," in point of fact, he was probably in St. Patrick's Cathedral, the largest neogothic cathedral in North America.

21. It should be stressed that in my view, the project of revitalizing a Christian culture is not undertaken simply for an apologetic gain but also with the expectation that the best aspects of culture serve as preparatory adornments for the New Jerusalem. In that broader sense, the apologetic benefit is merely a natural byproduct.

I would direct them to C. S. Lewis's important address "Learning in War-time."[22] Just maybe we could have both.

The Short View: The Role of Arguments

As important as the broad cultural project is, we should also continue to pursue excellence in philosophical argumentation while recognizing that the effectiveness of arguments must be assessed on broader criteria than logical validity and soundness alone.

I was brought to consider this point a few years ago when I brought a seminary class to hear William Lane Craig speak at Mill Woods Pentecostal Assembly in Edmonton, Alberta. In about thirty minutes, Craig charged through five arguments for God's existence (or, rather, four arguments and a testimony). Although my students had to work to keep up with Craig's pace, they managed to grasp most of what Craig said. But as I looked around the auditorium it was clear that most people were *not* tracking with the arguments. And this is hardly surprising. After all, it seems a bit unrealistic to expect someone without philosophical training to grasp the impossibility of traversing an actual infinite in five minutes. But then, what was the point of the talk if not to give people arguments?

And then it occurred to me that perhaps the primary point of this talk was not to inform the laity of the kalam and cosmic fine-tuning arguments, but rather to let them know that there *are* powerful arguments for Christianity *and* impressive intellectuals who can articulate them. Perhaps for many people knowing this alone is enough. One could understand this in terms of credibility/rationality,[23] but one might also find this information as contributing to the overall plausibility of the faith.

In short, Christianity does not seem so ridiculous when you realize that there are academics like Craig who can cogently articulate reasons to believe in the existence of God and resurrection of Christ. Indeed, the plausibility of Christianity is increased simply by knowing that many leading philosophers are Christians (e.g., Marilyn McCord Adams, William

---

22. Lewis, "Learning in War-time."

23. For instance, we could have a communal form of "warrant transfer" in which one might hold a belief despite prima facie defeaters for the belief, based on the fact that someone else within one's epistemic community is aware of a defeater for the defeater. Stephen Wykstra proposes something like this in "Toward a Sensible Evidentialism."

Alston, Michael Dummett, Alasdair MacIntyre, Alvin Plantinga, Merold Westphal). One might thus surmise that the more Christians succeed in reestablishing themselves as leaders in their respective academic fields, the more they will contribute both to the wider cultural renewal and to the background plausibility and credibility of the Christian faith.

Thus far we have focused on the question of plausibility. Within this context, we have treated arguments as cultural furniture that contribute to a space of plausibility within which Christianity is considered to be a live option. Still, as I noted above with the conversion of Antony Flew, arguments continue to play a crucial role in providing a rational ground for Christian faith. However, the conventional assessment of an argument's success in terms of validity and soundness[24] is clearly too narrow.

By analogy, it is too narrow to assume as many have, that the worth of a biblical translation is measured by the extent to which it reproduces the words of the original languages. On such a criterion, translations that sacrifice nuance for a simplified vocabulary (Good News Translation), or which are highly idiomatic (*The Message*), are necessarily inferior. But as Gordon Fee and Mark L. Strauss point out, this simple criterion misses the important place of the reader in translation assessment:

> One reader picks up a formal equivalent version and reads Paul's letter to the Romans, understanding about 50 percent of what he reads. Another person picks up a children's version like the NIrV and reads the same letter, comprehending about 95 percent of what she reads. One might well ask, who walks away with a greater knowledge of God's Word? The point is that whatever inadequacies an idiomatic version may have are far outweighed by the benefits of hearing and comprehending God's Word.[25]

If we take Fee and Strauss seriously, then it is worth asking whether the Gideons ought to replace the fossilized edition of the KJV that sits unread in thousands of hotel rooms with a translation more likely to be picked up. Granted *The Message* sacrifices words like "propitiation," but at least people would be more likely to crack the spine.

---

24. A valid argument is one where the conclusion follows logically from the premises, whereas a sound argument has both validity and truth.

25. Fee and Strauss, *How to Choose a Translation*, 41. The NIrV is the readers version of the NIV, a version that is simplified for children and ESL readers (like the Good News Translation).

The same observation can be made with respect to argument. Though validity and soundness are important, if you are concerned to convert others to your viewpoint, then this is clearly not enough. In short, what good is a sound argument that nobody understands, or one that invokes derision because it appears ridiculous? George Mavrodes thus recognized in his classic *Belief in God* that it is inadequate to assess arguments for God's existence in terms of validity and soundness alone.[26] As he puts it, arguments are *person relative*, and thus we ought to consider the value of an argument with respect to a particular audience. As such, he proposes a focus that looks beyond validity and soundness to include other considerations as well with the end goal of winning adherents as well as arguments.

Mavrodes develops this line of thought further in his essay "On the Very Strongest Arguments," in which he considers the properties of a good argument.[27] In addition to the standard criterion that an argument be compelling (based on validity), he adds that the best arguments are *accessible* (for what good is a compelling proof if only the logician who originally devised it is able to understand it?) and *attractive*. Though C. S. Lewis may not have matched a contemporary philosopher like Elizabeth Anscombe for logical prowess, he was head and shoulders above his peers in crafting arguments of accessibility and attractiveness.

Conclusion

I have sought to argue that Christian philosophers occasionally win logical battles at the expense of the war over the plausibility of the faith in Western culture. Thus in order to return Christianity to the place of being a live intellectual option, we need to recognize that rational discourse is intricately interwoven with a broad range of non-rational factors (e.g., psychological, sociological, political, hamartiological).[28] Thus, Christians should shift from focusing on logical argumentation to the multidimensional needs and concerns of persons, situating the rightful and strategic

26. Interestingly, Mavrodes points out that one could have a valid and sound argument and yet have gained nothing by way of knowledge; see *Belief in God*, 29–31.

27. Mavrodes, "On the Very Strongest Arguments."

28. See John Calvin's description of the noetic effects of sin in *Institutes of the Christian Religion*, III.2.10.

use of arguments within the broader context and concern for cultural renewal.

But thus far we have focused on the persons who are skeptical of the faith and thus remain to be convinced. Equally important are the persons who are to share the gospel, which brings me back to Webber's emphasis on love. To take one example, though I find myself irritated by comparisons between the Christian God and the flying spaghetti monster, I recognize nonetheless that bearing up under the barbs of scathing parody, and even adding a self-deprecating note to the chorus, contributes in its own modest way to the plausibility of Christianity. Indeed, it may be precisely in those moments when the rhetoric is most intense and the derision most palpable, that a soft answer which turns away wrath will manifest the most persuasive argument of all.

16

The King of the Mice:
An Earnest Fable for My Atheist Friends

Larry Gilman

Once upon a time, there was a schoolmaster in a village near Bremen. He was a well-read man, conversant with the arts and sciences, and his life would have been entirely pleasant except that he lived next door to a certain old woman who sold fish in the street. She stank and her apron was smeared with fish guts; her diction was coarse, her opinions grotesque. She was mean-spirited, too, and could often be heard crying that this or that person would be lashed to the bone in the town square if she had her way. Her stall was right by the schoolmaster's door, so whenever he went in or out he had to endure her presence.

Everything about the fishmonger offended the schoolmaster, but what enraged him most was her practice of intercepting students on their way to his rooms for instruction in natural philosophy. She would block the door at the bottom of his stair with her dirty bulk and regale the children with the most astonishing lies. Once, he heard her claiming that the sun is a ball of burning wax carried on a dwarf's back; another time, that the mice have a language of their own and a king and a parliament behind the wall; and so on.

One day, two of the schoolmaster's students were late for their lessons. Wondering why, he went down into the street. There was the fishmonger, brandishing a dead fish in the air as she shouted at his amazed students that women are got with child by eating herring.

"You fool!" he laughed, and the people in the street laughed too.

The fishmonger turned on him. "Laugh, wiseacre," she hissed. "Laugh! But God will pay you for that word."

He laughed again and called his students up into his office. What nobody noticed was that both times the schoolmaster laughed, he shrank slightly—just a hair's width, but so it was. And as he shrank, so she grew.

After this incident, the schoolmaster began to make a point of jeering at the fishmonger every time he went in or out. Sometimes, burning with the thought of her grossness and lying folly, he would even leave his book and go downstairs for the sole purpose of jeering at her before the crowd. But every time he laughed, he shrank and she grew.

Soon he was the smallest, shrillest man in the village and she was the biggest, boldest woman. And still he laughed and still she scolded, and still he shrank and still she grew.

Eventually the schoolmaster was no bigger than your thumb and had difficulty even reading his books. It took all his strength to open one, and he could only read a page by running back and forth along the lines of print. One day at the time appointed for receiving students, he heard the fishmonger's voice outside his window again, bellowing like an ox, "Two and two make five! The Earth is flat!"

In a rage, the schoolmaster hopped down from his reading desk, scampered to the door, squeezed under it, and jumped down the steps one by one. Finally he stood on the street before the fishmonger and her audience of gaping children.

He shook his tiny fist and squeaked his rage up at the mountain of filthy, ignorant fat above him. The fishmonger looked down with a greasy grin of triumph.

"Who's the fool now?" she shrieked. "Who will take your students? And who will stand behind your desk to teach them? And who will replace you on the town council and cast a vote with the burghers? I will!" And she raised one great foot above the schoolmaster to smash him flat.

He fled for a little hole in the wall as the fishmonger stomped after him in hot pursuit, her every step shaking the ground, and dodged into it just as her heel crashed down on the cobbles outside.

He stood gasping and shaking for a minute in the darkness between the walls. When his eyes had learned to see, he saw around him the glinting of a thousand bright eyes like stars.

"The King, the King!" cried many high voices. "He has come at last!"

The mice carried him off to their parliament and set him up on a throne of dirty toothpicks. They put a bottle cap on his head for a crown and a burnt-out match in his hand for a scepter and made him give them orders. "Do this, do that," he would say, sick to his soul of the meaningless game, but they would not feed him otherwise. And joyfully they obeyed him—any command at all but to set him free.

There behind the wall he lived out his life, and never laughed again.

As for the fishmonger, she was as good as her word. She took the schoolmaster's former students and taught them her folly from behind his very desk, and she took his seat on the town council and cast a vote with the burghers and became a power in the land. And Folly, they say, rules that country to this day.

17

Faith as the Art of the Possible:
Invigorating Religious Tradition in an Amnesiac Society

RONALD A. KUIPERS

"Are You Religious?"

"Are you religious?" she asked me point blank.

Up until that moment, I thought we had been having a casual conversation. That is, we were not having a serious discussion about the meaning of life, or sharing intimate personal witness and testimony. Our conversation, at least until that moment, could only be described as small talk.

She asked me, "What do you do?"

"I'm nearing completion of a PhD in philosophy," I replied.

"At the University of Toronto?"

"No, at the Institute for Christian Studies (ICS)," I said.

As usual, the burden then fell upon me to fill the yawning chasm of dumbfounded silence this reply often produces between myself and my interlocutor. Normally in this situation, I offer a brief description of the ICS, which, given the unique nature of this small, independent, Christian graduate school of interdisciplinary philosophy and theology, is no easy task. In fact, by the time I finish giving such a description, it is not uncommon for my now somewhat puzzled conversation partner to have convinced himself or herself that, at such a school, I could only be training for a career in the ministry. (Even a close hockey buddy of mine still confuses me for a minister from time to time, but I forgive him.) This time, however, the question that followed my explanation was simply, "Are you religious?"

I must confess to having stumbled over this seemingly straightforward question. One might even say that perhaps no simpler question could be asked of a philosopher schooled in the Reformational tradition of Christian philosophy, one whose mentor, Hendrik Hart, worked hard and effectively to pass along the deep impress of H. Evan Runner's maxim, "Life is Religion."[1] Still, I clearly remember balking at the question. It ran afoul of the social truism that at informal social gatherings one should refrain from asking personal questions about politics or religion. Generally, I'm not a stickler for such social conventions, but, after all, I had only recently met this person.

But my biggest stumbling block to answering this question with a simple, unqualified "Yes" was, and still is, that these days I am never sure exactly what I am being asked to affirm or deny. Several questions run through my mind at this point: What does she mean by "religious"? Will she impute any undesirable character traits to me if I answer yes? Which exemplars typify the category for her—Ghandi, Theresa, and Romero, or Dobson, Falwell, and LaHaye? Is she a disciple of Richard Dawkins, just waiting to pounce all over my "God delusion"? Or is she a fellow Christian, or a person committed to some other faith, someone searching for solidarity in a secularized liberal society where opportunities for open, public discussion of one's religious convictions are few and far between? There is simply no way of knowing in advance where she is coming from, unless, at the risk of seeming rather obtuse (or, perhaps, like a philosopher), I first ask her for too many explanations and qualifications concerning what is, after all, a pretty direct question.

Perhaps, it occurred to me, I could, before simply answering her question, offer some qualifications of my own. For example, I could take the time to explain to her that, not only am I religious, but I have been trained in an intellectual tradition that rejects the Enlightenment belief in the possibility of religious neutrality, that is, of anyone not being religious in some sense. The lives of all persons, and not just the lives of those who commit themselves to a particular religious tradition, are rooted in a trust-orientation, an "ultimate concern" that is itself not rationally grounded or groundable, and therefore, not religiously neutral. Would

1. See Runner, *Relation of the Bible to Learning*. See also Nielsen and Hart, *Search for Community in a Withering Tradition*. Hart puts forward a compelling case for the inescapability of religious starting points in philosophical argumentation, not to mention life as a whole.

such a reply, however, not simply amount to a grand and overly precious evasion of this deceptively simple question, akin to a description of the night when all cows are black?

In this space, I want to explore the possibility of providing an affirmative answer to this woman's question, which I have discovered is not really a simple matter at all. In so doing, I hope to offer some suggestions concerning what it might mean, and more importantly, what it perhaps ought to mean, for a Christian such as myself to affirm his faith in a pluralistic, differentiated society like ours, one that is deeply damaged, yet one that is neither hopeless nor without possibilities for significant healing and restorative transformation.

My strategy will be to work backward from the title of the essay by first providing a critical description of our society—that is, a Western, post-industrial, consumer-capitalist society steeped in ecological crisis to which I have given the adjective *amnesiac*. From there, I will discuss what it might mean to partake in and pass along a religious tradition in such a society, a religious tradition that, when healthy, invigorates its members for the ongoing task of healing and restoring that society, and, when unhealthy, itself stands in need of such invigoration. Membership in such a tradition, I will finally suggest, can, at its best, inspire a kind of faith that I will describe as "the art of the possible." Such a faith can give those graced by it the courage to shape their lives in relation to the mysterious contours of what the agrarian poet, novelist, and philosopher Wendell Berry calls "the human definition."[2] Although such an art of living does indeed call upon us to relinquish the push for cosmic mastery that has come to dominate our species, such a responsive, creaturely life involves much more than merely acquiescing before some authoritarian limit. Crafting such a life should be understood, instead, as a work of love that makes space for the beloved, a life that readies a place that may be graced by new and unpredictable redemptive possibility.

Fragmented Meaning in an Amnesiac Society

Our society is deeply marked by the historical processes of secularization. According to Max Weber, "The fate of our times is characterized by rationalization and intellectualization and, above all, by the 'disenchantment

2. See Berry, *Unsettling of America*, 94.

of the world." In place of a religiously charged cosmos, these modern processes of rationalization have ushered in a world we now consider fundamentally "knowable." Modern people no longer live out their lives in relation to "mysterious incalculable forces," but instead arm themselves with the conviction that "one can, in principle, master all things by calculation." According to Weber, modern people look to "technical means and calculations" to achieve the mastery over nature that, according to him, a more primitive humanity once sought by entreating magical or mysterious spiritual powers.[3] Now, while the predictions of religion's imminent demise following in the wake of Weber's pioneering work have proved to be an exaggeration,[4] his characterization of modernity still rings true to those who live in the modern (and one is tempted to say "wild") West. At the very least, his work astutely marks the historical emergence of a new world-shaping spiritual force on the global scene, and that force is humankind itself, including and especially our relatively newfound powers of scientific discovery and technological manipulation of the natural world. The fact that today we can speak so easily about something called a "human ecological footprint" tells us something about the strength and dynamism of this force.

The French sociologist of religion Danièle Hervieu-Léger describes modern societies as "societies of change," which she distinguishes from "societies of memory." According to Hervieu-Léger, "The affirmation of the autonomous individual, the advance of rationalization breaking up the 'sacred canopies,' and the process of institutional differentiation denote the end of societies based on memory." Change societies, which neglect to care for the continued creative reception of any collective memory, corrode any traditional context in which one might receive and participate in "individual and collective systems of meaning."[5] For Hervieu-Léger, "[T]he diminution of memory involves the erosion of the imaginative grasp of continuity," which we require in our struggle to achieve a meaningful human identity. Modernity's hyperindividualism can thus be seen as both a

3. Weber, "Science as Vocation," 155, 139. Whether he shares the opinion or is merely describing it, Weber here effectively illustrates the rather presumptuous modern understanding of premodern religious and ritual practice as so many versions of the same mistake, that is, as so many forms of failed empirical science. For a criticism of this understanding, see Wittgenstein, *Remarks on Fraser's Golden Bough*.

4. See Berger, *Desecularization of the World*.

5. Hervieu-Léger, *Religion as a Chain of Memory*, 127, 129.

consequence of and a contributor to this loss of memory. In an amnesiac society, people are left to their own devices to cobble together what meaning they can amid the fragments that are still available to them, a situation that plays right into the hands of the economic imperatives of a consumer-capitalist economy, which trades mainly in the immediate gratification of individual desire. The "individualistic pressure for immediacy," Hervieu-Léger suggests, "has finally achieved the expulsion of memory from society, so completing a process which began with modernization."[6]

One comes across a rather stark and chilling example of this sort of hyperindividualistic desertion of memory in the vision for a posthuman future that is now being promoted by a loose, but culturally influential, collection of highly gifted and motivated inventors, computer scientists, and geneticists. Take the case of Rodney Brooks, robotics pioneer and director of Massachusetts Institute of Technology's Computer Science and Artificial Intelligence Laboratory. Brooks welcomes the prospect that human technological progress now stands at the cusp of replacing our very humanity. "There is no need to worry about mere robots taking over from us," he explains. "We will be taking over from ourselves. The distinction between us and robots is going to disappear."[7] Not only does Brooks insist that "those of us alive today, over the course of our lifetimes, will morph ourselves into machines,"[8] a quick trip over to his Web site reveals that he doesn't even think that human beings in their current "unmorphed" state are anything but highly complex machines. The lure of advanced robotics, then, for someone like Brooks, can only be the promise of making ourselves into better machines than the ones we already are.

In the book *Enough: Staying Human in an Engineered Age*, Bill McKibben draws our attention to the beguiling way in which this techno-topian vision of a posthuman future brings together a certain self-loathing for the kind of creatures we are, with a "never-look-back" optimism concerning the inevitability of this kind of technological "progress"; "human beings simply must push on," always expanding their powers. As McKibben summarizes, "In 1492, Columbus sailed the ocean blue; in 1969 Neil Armstrong took 'one giant leap for mankind'; and sometime

---

6. Ibid., 137–38.

7. Brooks, *Flesh and Machines*, 53; cited in McKibben, *Enough*, 99.

8. Brooks, *Flesh and Machines*, 212; cited in McKibben, *Enough*, 68.

very soon there will be a baby born with improved hardware. By our nature we must crack the nucleus of the cell."[9]

Clearly, this vision of our human future takes modern amnesia to a whole new level. Not only does such a vision fail to credit any traditional understanding of the human definition, it actively toys with the possibility of changing that definition forever, and as McKibben warns, it could in the process destroy what it means to be human at all. Yet before we as a culture back ourselves into a future that we cannot undo, we might want to heed Wendell Berry's advice, and for once restrain the use of our machines. Says Berry (writing in the mid-1970s):

> Much as we long for infinities of power and duration, we have no evidence that these lie within our reach, much less within our responsibility. It is more likely that we will have either to live within our limits, within the human definition, or not live at all. And certainly the true knowledge of these limits and of how to live within them is the most comely and graceful knowledge that we have, the most healing and the most whole.[10]

Invigorating Religious Tradition

Where do religious traditions, and in particular the family of Christian traditions, stand in relation to this heady modern context? The story, I'm afraid, is far from clear, and it is far from reassuring. Clearly, the vitality and robustness of religious traditions have also suffered from the same fragmentation and loss of memory that infects the rest of modern society. According to Hervieu-Léger's account, in which memory and its modern corrosion play a central role in her sociological definition of religion, "The question of secularization here takes on a new form, namely that of the possibility, and plausibility, of a group being able, within a context of memory reduced to fragments and made instantaneous, to recognize itself as a link in a chain of belief," one that has been "entrusted with the task of extending that chain into the future."[11] Such is the challenge she

---

9. McKibben, *Enough*, 202. Jürgen Habermas puts forward a trenchant critique of the scientistic anthropology that informs people like Brooks. See Habermas, "Faith and Knowledge," esp. 331–32.

10. Berry, *Unsettling of America*, 94.

11. Hervieu-Léger, *Religion as a Chain of Memory*, 130.

places before those among us today who still wish to pattern our lives according to the contours provided by a particular religious tradition.

The difficulty here lies in the fact that often these traditions themselves have become forgetful, aligning themselves too readily with the prevailing individualism and consumer mentality that dominates the modern world. As Hervieu-Léger reports, "[S]tudies made of religious beliefs and of the substance of the new religiosity of Christian persuasion in the developed world all stress the place given to themes of self-realization and personal achievement in this world."[12] Too often, it seems, today's Christians let themselves be little more than religious customers, shopping for an individualistic version of "health and wealth" religion.[13]

In direct contestation to this understanding of the Christian message, the secular philosopher Jürgen Habermas reminds us that "the biblical vision of salvation does not mean simply liberation from individual guilt, but also implies collective liberation from situations of misery and oppression."[14] Have we already forgotten so much that we require such a reminder from a secular philosopher?

There is reason to hope that things are not yet that dire. For example, many thoughtful Christians have begun to question individualistic interpretations of their faith. I have already mentioned Wendell Berry's call for us to restrain our use of machines and to instead embrace life within the human limits that give it meaning and open it up to graceful possibility. A rather lonely voice for some time, Berry's message is starting to reach a steadily growing audience, a fact that gives me hope that Christians, in particular, have not severed all memorial connection with the wisdom inherent in their tradition.

In *The Paradise of God: Renewing Religion in an Ecological Age*, Norman Wirzba laments that "we do not pay attention to the remnants of traditions that hold within themselves the patient accumulation of

---

12. Ibid., 138.

13. I am here reminded of Theodor W. Adorno's rather pessimistic description of what has become of religion in this modern context: "Religion is on sale, as it were. It is cheaply marketed in order to provide one more so-called irrational stimulus among many others by which the members of a calculating society are calculatingly made to forget the calculation under which they suffer" ("Theses upon Art and Religion Today," 678).

14. Habermas, "Israel or Athens," 79.

wisdom necessary for a sustainable life."[15] But the fact remains that such remnants are still there for us to heed, should we care to take notice of them. As McKibben reminds us, Berry's call for restraint in our use of technology is a case in point:

> [T]hough it galls the apostles of technology, this idea of restraint comes in large measure from our religious heritage. Not the religious heritage of literalism and fundamentalism and pie-in-the-sky-when-you-die. The scientists may have drowned the miracle-working sky gods with their five-century flood of data. Copernicus and Darwin did deprive us of our exalted place in the universe. But this older, deeper, more integral religious idea survives. . . . [I]t has persisted for millennia through its insistence that instead of putting ourselves at the center, we need to move a little to the side.[16]

While this religious memory survives, it has perhaps never been more vulnerable. It is clear to me, however, that, not only must it continue to survive; it must also be invigorated to the extent that it can become a new rallying point for global human solidarity. That we may only be left with fragments of our religious past, I do not presume to say with any degree of certainty. Yet these memories, as "fragmentary, diffuse, and disassociated" as they might be, still hold the promise that "something of collective identification, on which the production and reproduction of social bonds depends, can be saved."[17] It is in light of the current imperative for worldwide humanity to come together and embrace life within the human definition that I wish to understand faith as the art of the possible.

Faith as the Art of the Possible

In arguing against the malaise of modern amnesia, I do not intend to recommend a nostalgic longing for the recapitulation of a vanished, romanticized past (that perhaps never existed in the first place). The danger of modern amnesia, rather, lies in the way it ignores the human condition of existing, to borrow a phrase from Hannah Arendt, "between past and future." Although Arendt affirms that "the thread of tradition is broken

15. Wirzba, *Paradise of God*, 166.
16. McKibben, *Enough*, 208, 210.
17. Hervieu-Léger, *Religion as a Chain of Memory*, 141.

and that we shall not be able to renew it," she nevertheless counsels those who would dismantle tradition to "be careful not to destroy the 'rich and strange,' the 'coral' and the 'pearls,' which can probably be saved only as fragments."[18]

In a similar way, Paul Ricoeur affirms this temporal feature of the human condition. For Ricoeur, the condition of "being-affected-by-a-past" forms a pair with the futural intending of a "horizon of expectation." That is, our hopes and expectations relative to the future inform and thus have repercussions on our reinterpretations of the past. One major repercussive effect, he suggests, is to open up "forgotten possibilities, aborted potentialities, repressed endeavors in the supposedly closed past." The same effect occurs in the opposite direction: through our attempt to interpret a textual tradition inherited from a distant past we create a space in which to subject our present reality to critical scrutiny, and thus, imagine a better future. Following these fragments of memory may "lead us back to those moments of the past where the future was not yet decided," and in so doing, make room for new possibility: "It is through this interplay of expectation and memory that the utopia of a reconciled humanity can come to be invested in effective-history."[19] Truth and reconciliation processes like the one recently tried in South Africa provide one example of such interplay: here the people of South Africa allowed their hope for social healing to be informed by the active memory of a religious testimony, which suggests forgiveness as a historically effective alternative to vengeance.[20]

We may live in dark times. This does not mean, however, that there is no light at all. This possibility, too, is affirmed by the social philosopher Theodor Adorno, who is not generally given to excessive optimism

---

18. See Arendt, *Life of the Mind*, 1:202–13, 212. Arendt takes the images of coral and pearls from the following passage in Shakespeare's *The Tempest* (I.2): "Full fathom five thy father lies, / Of his bones are coral made, / Those are pearls that were his eyes. / Nothing of him that doth fade / But doth suffer a sea-change / Into something rich and strange."

19. Ricoeur, *Time and Narrative*, 227–28; see also Ricoeur, "Hermeneutics and the Critique of Ideology," 306: "[N]othing is more deceptive than the alleged antinomy between an ontology of prior understanding and an eschatology of freedom. We have encountered these false antinomies elsewhere: as if it were necessary to choose between reminiscence and hope! In theological terms, eschatology is nothing without the recitation of acts of deliverance from the past."

20. See Helmick and Petersen, *Forgiveness and Reconciliation*.

concerning "a wholly enlightened earth" whose "light" radiates only "triumphant calamity."[21] As opposed to this pseudo-light, Adorno affirms the vulnerable existence of differing shards that still manage to pierce our darkness: "Good," he tells us, "is what wrenches itself free, finds a language, opens its eyes. In its condition of wrestling free, it is interwoven in history that, without being organized unequivocally toward reconciliation, in the course of its movement allows the possibility of redemption to flash up."[22]

Arendt locates this redemptive possibility in the human capacity to initiate, to make something new in the space of life between past and future. She describes this feature of our condition, which she calls "natality," as "the miracle that saves the world." People, she says, "though they must die, are not born in order to die but in order to begin. . . . Only the full experience of this capacity can bestow upon human affairs faith and hope."[23] Religious traditions, including the family of traditions collected under the umbrella of Christianity, still know something about such faith and hope, as Arendt herself affirms.[24] For a Christian thinker like Wirzba, the full experience of our capacity for acting, for initiating something new, is rooted in a profession of covenant partnership with the Maker. As such, he would have us understand hope as "more than simply the actualization of past or present potential," for to "configure hope on a continuum with a sordid and destructive past," and thus to "base hope on potential as we currently see it," is to "undermine" it. Hope, for Wirzba, is instead "steeped in the possibility of God to make something new."[25]

21. Horkheimer and Adorno, *Dialectic of Enlightenment*, 1.

22. Adorno, "Progress," 148.

23. Arendt, *Human Condition*, 246–47.

24. Arendt's chapter on "Action" in *The Human Condition* ends with these words: "It is this faith in and hope for the world that found perhaps its most glorious and most succinct expression in the few words with which the Gospels announced their 'glad tidings': 'A child has been born unto us.'" In addition to crediting this historical tradition with originating the notions of forgiveness and promise, she also claims that "[a]ction is, in fact, the one miracle-working faculty of man, as Jesus of Nazareth, whose insights into this faculty can be compared in their originality and unprecedentedness with Socrates' insights into the possibilities of thought, must have known very well when he likened the power to forgive to the more general power of performing miracles, putting both on the same level and within the reach of man" (ibid., 246–47).

25. Wirzba, *Paradise of God*, 54.

In this space, between a memorial past and an anticipated future, Christians may respond to the creaturely call to faithfully image their Maker. Along these lines, the Christian philosopher James Olthuis encourages us to understand our human creaturely being as something that is both a gift and a call.[26] Anticipating God's future redemption as promised in Scripture, an act in which remembrance and hope come together, we will come to embrace the gift of life housed within the human definition. Such an embrace, in turn, also becomes an affirmative response to the call to make room for, and thus help to initiate, redemptive possibilities that will steer us away from the fatalistic acceptance of our damaged present that is currently prevailing in modern society.

Should we care to think of God's creative act as the loving act through which God makes space for an other to be, this will determine our understanding of how we might best image God. In creating the world, God pulls back and limits Godself. God's creative act can be seen in this way as a paradigmatic act of love, for love makes room for the beloved to be. As creatures called to image such a loving Maker, our lives are to exhibit the same kind of love. By saying "enough," by saying, "this life as it has been given to me, though not perfect, is enough," we choose to embrace life within the human definition as it has been given to us by God. To limit ourselves in this way is also to engage in a similar act of loving space-making as the one God performed. Such divine imaging makes space for God to be a real presence in human life, and makes space in our hearts for a broken world that we may once again experience as, in the words of the Victorian poet Gerard Manley Hopkins, charged with "God's grandeur." Should we choose to embrace our liberating limits, we will see that, for all its "trade" and "toil," deep in every detail of creation "there lives the dearest freshness." With Hopkins, we may even kindle hope for a new morning, confident that the Holy Ghost broods over our bent world "with warm breast and with ah! bright wings."[27]

Today's Christian, I submit, needs to consider deeply the possibilities afforded by understanding one's faith in such terms. Can we come to understand our faith in terms of the sacrifice and courage that living such a God-imaging life requires? Will we open ourselves to the grace we must receive in order to be able to hit that human note with something

---

26. See Olthuis, "Be(com)ing Humankind as Gift and Call."
27. Hopkins, "God's Grandeur."

that approaches perfect pitch? To speak personally for a moment, and to push this musical metaphor just a bit, I would like to say that, although I am afraid that my life will in some sense always be out of tune, or at the very least a repeated exercise in tuning and being attuned, I can at least gratefully say that I have come to have a much clearer sense of the divine song I want my heart to sing, of the divine dance in which I wish my life to take part.

I now see faith in terms of a life contoured by such an artful performance. My faith is shaped by the desire and the attempt to craft a life that, in love, embraces the human definition and, in making space for others, in preparing a place for them, is also a blessing to those others—that, to me, is what it means to describe faith as the art of the possible.

Am I religious? In hope, I answer: "Yes, I am."

18

Mystery and Mayhem: Reading Bulgakov's *The Master and Margarita* while Dating an Atheist in Seattle

Becky Crook

In the curdling heat of the summer of 2007, I went to Town Hall, Seattle's cultural watering hole, to whet my whistle at a lecture by Steven Pinker. Pinker is a renowned evolutionary psychologist and cognitive scientist whose work on language and cognition seeks to debunk certain myths about the mind. Among other things, Pinker believes that all of human behavior—including, morality, love, and free will—is reducible to the firing of neurons across synapses in the brain. In a 2002 interview with *Reason* magazine, Pinker posited:

> Neuroscience is showing that all aspects of mental life—every emotion, every thought pattern, every memory—can be tied to the physiological activity or structure of the brain. Cognitive science has shown that feats that were formerly thought to be doable by mental stuff alone can be duplicated by machines, that motives and goals can be understood in terms of feedback and cybernetic mechanisms, and that thinking can be understood as a kind of computation . . . So intelligence, which formerly seemed miraculous—something that mere matter could not possibly accomplish or explain—can now be understood as a kind of computation process.[1]

Now, I haven't got a bone to pick against chemical causes and reactions, which can be measured and observed for each thought and emotion, but I believe that these observations neither explain nor diminish the wonder of life's miracle. On the contrary, such scientific findings should naturally

---

1. Bailey and Gillespie, "Biology vs. the Blank Slate," ¶ 27.

elicit wonder and gratitude of those things that remain unpinpointed. And thus, the need to eliminate mystery from life, to laugh at it as though it were a silly outdated notion strikes me as odd. As Pinker spoke, the intellectual, mostly white and well-to-do crowd of Seattleites laughed knowingly at his every awe-bashing intonation.

At home, I tried to shake the disappointed feeling that I had returned with my thought bucket only half-full. The lecture brimmed with pithy cognitive-linguistic theories and riddles that were just smart enough to make a listener feel intelligent and superior. However, much of Pinker's talk felt vacuous, like a space into which were flicked little pieces of dry-wall or plaster filler. That is, there seemed to be nothing I could take home and apply in a lasting, meaningful, or colorful manner; there was nothing to chew on.

I wondered, is this what we've come to expect and consume—drywall and plaster? Empty half-truth?[2]

This type of enlightenment—one which seeks to reduce the fullness of reality to what is empirically verifiable and rationally explicable—removes from the cultural vocabulary a valuable sense of mystery, of something that exceeds our concepts and eludes our theoretical grasp. Such a reduction allows us only to talk about a chunk of what is real—the observable chunk. The other elements of our lives, hearts, world, spirit, and community become unspeakable and unrecognizable.

In turn, our words of science and reason, which should rightly be used to enhance and to fruitfully challenge the discourse of those myste-rious and unknowable things, are left instead to fill a space that they have neither the capacity nor the purpose to fill. Using science to describe what isn't primarily scientific is like dancing about architecture, like speaking with empty, plaster words.

At this point, like a bell in some little lobal section where reason isn't always straightforward, a poem by Wendell Berry struck my brain. He imagines a day when "ugliness is perfected in rubble," a world where "all the words . . . mean nothing." Berry suggests that the beauty inher-ent in our words is being hollowed out, reducing meaningful discourse about our spiritual experiences. He believes that in such a predicament

2. Steven Pinker is brilliant, and his work is incredible—especially his work on language acquisition and the mind. This is my gut reaction after hearing his lecture, a visceral experience that is quite different from reading about ideas in a book. My reaction has much to do with hearing him in the crowd at Town Hall.

we should "let silence / speak for us" so that we might regain our ability to recognize the unempirical truths, which, if we are humble and attentive, may then quietly venture out to reveal themselves to us.[3]

Humble attention is precisely what is lacking for the majority of characters in Michael Bulgakov's novel *The Master and Margarita,* which I was reading at the time of the Pinker lecture. Bulgakov's main characters don't take time for attention. They are set in their assumptions and rush hot-blooded through the narrative's violent, insane fiascos.

The novel opens benignly enough on a park bench near the water one hot evening as two prominent Muscovite writers argue about the best method for articulating Jesus's nonexistence—taken as a matter of indisputable fact by both men and by Moscow's public in general. Then, out of the blue, the devil appears to them both, interrupting their conversation and igniting a series of inexplicable events.

The devil! The devil comes to Moscow!

Satan appears as the shabby, somewhat lewd, conversationally unorthodox professor Woland, an expert in black magic who is—not surprisingly—delighted to find the city filled with atheists who deny the existence of God. But even the devil seems shocked and upset to find that as a result of this godless self-sufficiency, Moscow's populace cannot recognize his identity.

All hell breaks loose. The devil professor turns the city upside down, yet no one recognizes him. The city is so wrapped up in its self-created image of scholarship, reason, jazz, and elaborate atheistic theologies that its citizens cannot recognize something contradictory, even if it's the Fury of Hell himself.

Indeed, the only characters who surmise Woland's true identity are eventually checked in to a psychiatric clinic. In a world that discounts God and the devil, any contrary assertion is considered insane.

And thus, violence and disorder spread through the city, and all the time, its citizens can't name what is happening. What happened to our palatable reason, our plaster and drywall? Why can't we define and control this situation?

Nowhere is this desire for the certainty of reason more obvious in the novel than in the Black Magic Exposé that Woland enacts as an exclusive, one-day-only performance.

---

3. Berry, *Given Poems,* 128.

The audience (as white, intellectual, and well-to-do as ever I saw in Seattle's Town Hall) expects that Woland will exhibit the secret slights of hand behind his magic, only to find, in a clever trick of irony, that it is their own attachment to certainty and their stubborn inability to appreciate the miraculous which is exposed. Woland gives them magic but no explanation: he rains money and fancy clothes down on the audience and then watches appalled as the crowd jostles for the goods, revealing simultaneously their materialistic values and lack of appropriate awe for wonder. Afterward, the fancy clothes disappear and the money is turned into foreign notes. Naked and in possession of illegal currencies, the show-goers are promptly arrested in a debacle that uncovers the ultimate uncertainty of tangible, material reality and questions the definition of "indecency."

In the midst of the outrageous hubbub, Woland wonders whether humanity can reasonably expect to be in control and certain about anything:

> If there is no God, then, the question is who is in control of man's life and the whole order of things on earth? . . . In order to be in control, you have to have a definite plan for at least a reasonable period of time. So how, may I ask, can man be in control if he can't even draw up a plan for a ridiculously short period of time, say a thousand years, and is moreover unable to ensure his own safety for even the next day? . . . Yes, man is mortal, but that isn't so bad. What's bad is that sometimes he's unexpectedly mortal, that's the rub![4]

Clearly, in Bulgakov's topsy-turvy narrative, no one is less in control than those who think they have it all figured out—these unfortunate characters are met with beheadings, transfigurations, unreasonable instantaneous transportations, frauds, scams, disappearances, beatings, and jailings. Woland seems intent to disrupt every notion of order.

Yet in a strange paradox of the novel, all of the devil's attempts to stir up evil and disbelief somehow have the opposite effect, creating instead magic, beauty, and redemption. The reader, if she is a self-consciously spiritual person, is left to wonder whether it is in fact the devil who has appeared in Moscow, or whether it is some kind of mischievous manifestation of God—a sheep in wolf's clothing in a pen whose shepherds don't

4. Bulgakov, *Master and Margarita*, 8–9.

believe in the existence of sheep or wolves—who delights in turning all of our notions on their head. Or alternatively, is Bulgakov remarking upon the ability of the divine to fashion hope and goodness from disbelief and evil? God only knows!

There is, in the novel, one character whose complete awareness to the present allows her to immediately ascertain and recognize Satan. The novel's heroine, Margarita, is focused unwaveringly on her quest to be reunited with The Master, her lover, who like other discerning characters, resides in the insane asylum.

More than everyone else in the book, Margarita believes adamantly in the power and wonder of love, the power of something real beyond what is observable. When she meets Woland, she knows who and what he is, and accepts—without hesitation—a deal that will allow her to be reunited with The Master.

Anyone else, not recognizing the devil, would have found this Faustian offer ludicrous and unacceptable (or straightjacket-worthy)—a fool's hope—but Margarita seizes the gift, knowing that when the promise of happiness is offered, only a fool would question the existence of the extended hands. What matters is only this unreasonable gift and the active belief that one can, as if by magic, accept it. This is what makes Margarita the most powerful and clear-eyed character in the entire blood-broiling mess. She alone abandons herself to the mystery of the evil (or good?) deity because she is the only character not bound to the limits of the explicable.

And I wonder if it wasn't some devilish slight of fate when, just after I finished reading *The Master and Margarita*, and just after I'd heard Pinker's scientistic sermon, I sat one warm summer evening on a bench overlooking the water, as my atheist boyfriend told me that our ten-day relationship was over, because he just couldn't date someone who believed in God.

I looked at the sky twinkling above—us a pair of specks on a bench—and at the hundreds of dancing reflections in the water, all moving in random which-ways, every moment changing and every moment only to exist in that exact state for once in all eternity—and I asked him: "Why is it that you think I believe in God?" I tried to recall the past two weeks—had we discussed our theological beliefs? Had I unwittingly hummed "Jesus Loves Me" when washing the dishes?

"I know you believe in God because you practice gratitude."

This may have been the most notable breakup I've had, if only because it produced the opposite effect than what might have been expected. I found the statement not only an enormous—if inadvertent—compliment, but also an exhilarating, incredible tribute.

He's right. He's right! The devil take me if I am not grateful for this air that fills my lungs, for the water that sates my thirst, for this opportunity to exist as a speck on a bench in late summer in the middle of a vast universe. The devil take me if I don't grab hold of this gift with both hands, all the while yelling "Thank you! Thank you! Thank you!" to the unexplained hands that have given it to me—devil or divine, mischief-maker or do-gooder—why quarrel about their existence? What's important is that they exist to offer this beauty around me, and also that I exist—for some reason, maybe even for no reason that exists within reason, and god, am I grateful.

I don't think my new ex-boyfriend had anticipated this reaction. I was smiling and full of life, ready to hop onto a flying pig or ride a handbasket off to god-knows-where. I was so astonished by his admission that gratitude and faith went hand in hand, and that he could, in one fell swoop, refuse to take hold of both. How could he willingly give up that acceptance of something wonderful, just because he couldn't understand the where-from or why of it? He didn't seem able to recognize what was behind the incredible folly or madness or divinity or devilishness or magic—call it what you will—that was in me. Or maybe I should say that I was in It.

I was Bulgakov's Margarita, naked and supremely grateful and happy, and he was the fully clothed cynic, wanting something more but only seeing ideas that confine themselves to the narrow bridge of reason stretching out like a splinter into our universe.

Then I felt sorry for him, and for all the characters in Bulgakov's novel, whose philosophical muesli consists only of the flakes of truth that can be logically defined, without the fruit and honey of wonder. I can only hope that there is a gentle redemption for the cynics too, as there seems to be eventually in *The Master and Margarita*, and that disorder is somehow mysteriously transformed into beauty at the very end. I am so grateful for flavors that are ineffable, for the incarnational chewiness of miracle, and the experiences that escape definition. They drive me to silently view our universe in awe and gratitude, for the wholeness of all that exists—known and unknown—and to accept and embrace that gift as it carries me—where?— God only knows!

19

Why We Live in Community

CHRISTINE SINE

My husband Tom and I live in a small intentional community in Seattle, Washington, called the Mustard Seed House. We inhabit the middle floor of a triplex with a young family in the apartment above us and a young couple in the basement apartment below us. We get together at least once a week for dinner and sharing and once more for prayer, and we garden together once a month. We are keen on hospitality and have fun hosting people from around the world.

Recently we received a visit from Noemie, a young French woman who was traveling in North America to research sustainable forms of community living. Prior to visiting the Mustard Seed House she had already stayed at a cohousing community in Washington DC, an old-order Amish community in Pennsylvania, and an income-sharing commune in the woods of Virginia. She also met with Catholic Workers and young Christians from the New Monasticism movement who live in an intentional community.

Noemie did not grow up with a Christian background, but after her visits to these communities where she talked at length to community members about Christian faith and how to live out the gospel, she has become intrigued by the linkage between community and Christian living. Her recent experiences convinced her that the only way authentically to live out Christian faith is in community with others. She did not think that Christians all needed to live together in residential communities, but she did find that the more frequently they met together for meals, prayers, or activities, the more authentically their lives seemed to bear witness to the gospel message.

I agree with Noemie. The pressures of our individualistic, consumer-driven culture make many of us who call ourselves followers of Christ act like atheists. We may pray for a few minutes before we head off to work each morning and go to church on Sunday, but our faith has little impact on how we live the rest of the day. Our daily routines are increasingly not just disconnected from God's rhythms and purposes, but in competition with them.

For us, as for our secular neighbors, "Normal is getting dressed in clothes you buy for work, driving through traffic in a car you are still paying for, in order to get to the job that you need so you can pay for the clothes, car and the house that you leave empty all day in order to afford to live in it."[1]

Beyond Functional Atheism

New Testament scholar N. T. Wright asserts that Christianity's most distinctive idea is bodily resurrection. After his resurrection, Jesus was a flesh-and-blood person, and Wright contends that we will be too. He further argues that if we truly believe this, it will influence the way we live our lives now. If God intends to renew all of creation and all of life—a process already begun in the resurrection of Jesus—then our responsibility as Christians is to anticipate this renewal by refocusing our lives to work for hope and healing in today's world.

In his book *Surprised by Hope*, Wright asks, "So how can we learn to live as wide-awake people, as Easter people? If Calvary means putting to death things in your life that need killing off, if you are to flourish as a Christian and as a truly human being, then Easter should mean planting, watering, and training up things in your life (personal and corporate) that ought to be blossoming, filling the garden with color and perfume, and in due course, bearing fruit." He goes on to say that all the Gospels emphatically proclaim that "Jesus is risen, therefore God's new world has begun. Jesus is risen, therefore Israel and the world have been redeemed. Jesus is risen, therefore his followers have a new job to do. And what is that new job? To bring the life of heaven to birth in actual, physical earthly reality."[2]

1. De Graaf, *Affluenza*, 36.
2. Wright, *Surprised by Hope*, 255–57, 293.

At the core of our small Mustard Seed House community and its parent organization, Mustard Seed Associates, is our belief in this wild hope of the resurrection and our vision of God's eternal world as a place in which all of creation is restored and made whole. Through the redemptive work of Christ, we believe that one day, together with sisters and brothers of every culture and from every age, we will be made whole and live together in the love, joy, and mutual concern for God's original creation.

People have a variety of notions of Christian community. Most think of residential communities where twenty or thirty people live communally in a large house or on a farm. Others think of common-purse communities where members live in close proximity to each other and pool finances. Still others imagine monastic communities or religious orders that live by a common rule of life and take vows of simplicity and chastity but may not live in residential communities at all. We do not need to live together in residential communities in order to orient our lives around God's vision and purposes. To move beyond functional atheism and become the people God intends us to be, however, we do need to foster a sense of shared spirituality and commitment such as the monastic communities practice.

The idea of living in community or sharing a rule of life as an expression of our faith is not new. In fact, it can be traced right back to the beginning of Christianity. Early Christians believed that God comes to us in community—Father, Son, and Holy Spirit. They reasoned that as the essential nature of God is love and because it is impossible to practice love in isolation, the triune God must be a model of perfect community. Augustine believed that living together with others is necessary for the cultivation of spiritual formation and maturity, especially for the discipline of love: "Perfection in the spiritual life is impossible to attain as long as a person lives alone, for how can that person learn how to love?" The purpose of monastic communities became not just to establish a regimen of discipline, but also to nurture spiritual growth and "help facilitate the restoration of the image of God in sinful humans."[3] Similarly, the Celtic monasteries were understood to be "colonies of heaven, planted on earth to point as a sign and harbinger of the Kingdom that was yet to come."[4] They offered hospitality and provided a sacred space in which visitors

3. Sittser, *Water from a Deep Well*, 105, 103.

4. Bradley, *Colonies of Heaven*, 18.

could develop a rule of life with a regular rhythm of prayer and worship in the midst of their everyday activities. They also became educational and resource centers and the hubs out of which mission work was
accomplished.

Everything Must Change

Thinking of God as a community that consists not just of the Godhead
but also as the international community of God's people (and all creation) forces us to rethink everything. To become a follower of Christ
today does not necessarily mean that we all need to live together in a
residential community but it does mean reorienting our lives to more of
a community-oriented worldview. In this worldview, following Christ is
not about giving assent to a set of spiritual laws, but about being drawn
into a community of mutual love and relationship. We become part of
God's international community with sisters and brothers from every tribe
and nation, with the rich and the poor, the young and the old, the sick, the
lonely, the disabled, the homeless, the marginalized, and the abandoned.

If God does indeed come to us in community, then it is impossible to
reflect the image of God unless we too are willing to share life with others
in God's community. As Sittser reminds us:

> The people of God are privileged to belong to this commu-
> nity through the redemptive work of Christ and the indwelling
> power of the Holy Spirit. Such an experience of love inspired
> early Christians to share it with others. . . . they believed that Jesus
> Christ came to redeem and reclaim the fallen world, which in-
> volved even the most ordinary and routine matters of life, such as
> marriage and family, stewardship of money, treatment of friends
> and enemies, and daily conduct.[5]

To do mission work is no longer seen as fulfilling a desire to provide for
the spiritual and physical needs of others. Rather it is about learning to
love our neighbors as we do ourselves. It is recognizing that we cannot
share life with other members of God's international family as God intended unless we are in loving relationships and willing to enter into the
life journeys of others—to share their pain and their sorrows, to celebrate
their joys and their triumphs.

5. Sittser, *Water from a Deep Well*, 60.

Our understanding of spiritual disciplines must change too. Rather than seeing spiritual disciplines as individualistic and often legalistic observances of prayer and Bible study, they can be seen as the shared practices that renew our faith in God and God's kingdom vision for an eternal shalom world in which there will no longer be any pain or suffering or oppression or disease—as well as reconnecting us to others that hold the same beliefs. The term *spiritual discipline* can be applied to any habit performed regularly that strengthens our relationship to God, to each other, and to God's world.

Toward a Rule of Life

One way to establish new kingdom disciplines is by developing a rule of life. At the Mustard Seed House, we sense that God's Spirit is currently speaking through many voices about the need for a more embodied, incarnational faith, and we want to join in what God is doing. Developing a rule of life seems to be an important step in that process. According to the Northumbria Community, a rule of life says "'this is who we are, this is our story'; and it reminds us of those things God has put on our hearts, calling us back to our foundations."[6] A rule of life is a way to express our faith together as a community by establishing common practices that foster a sense of shared spirituality and commitment to God's kingdom purposes. It enables us to develop practices that connect the important basics of our faith to God, to God's worldwide community and to God's world. At the same time, it helps us to stand against the pressures of our consumer culture, which is constantly bombarding us with messages that are counter to God's values.

Mustard Seed Associates is working in this direction. We already share morning and evening prayer, a weekly community meal, and a monthly gardening day, and we are currently grappling with how each of us should be involved both in our local community and in global mission.

In a 24/7 world with no space for God or spirituality, we buy our freedom from work and business with some hard choices. How could we more intentionally commit ourselves to the community that God has made us a part of? We can start with small steps. I have a friend who

6. Miller, "Introduction," ¶1.

was so impacted by the story of Jesus preparing breakfast on the beach for his friends that he decided to bring coffee and rolls one morning a week to the staff at the local public school, which he saw as an essential element of his local community. This simple act has become an extremely important way of affirming the life and work of dedicated teachers who often feel unappreciated. What choices could we make that would enable us to move beyond functional atheism and face in a different direction— toward God and the values of God's eternal world?

20

Spring Prayer

Courtney Druz

It is easy to praise doubt
for most beauty wavers subtly,
sways, blossoms, dissolves in petals.

And it is easy to praise frailty
for most of us are frail
as a shimmering gorgeous beetle
ripe for the crushing.

But let me grow beyond the brittle carapace;
let me grow bones within
to leap like an ibex on the crags
with that sure footing which approaches flight.

Bibliography

Adorno, Theodor W. "Progress." In *Critical Models: Interventions and Catchwords*, translated by Henry W. Pickford, 143–60. New York: Columbia University Press, 1998.

———. "Theses upon Art and Religion Today." *Kenyon Review* 7:4 (1945) 677–82.

Ansell, Nicholas John. "It's About Time: Opening Our Reformational Paradigm to the Eschaton." Paper presented at the Institute for Christian Studies, Toronto, September 26, 2003.

Arendt, Hannah. *The Human Condition*. Chicago: University of Chicago Press, 1958.

———. *The Life of the Mind*. Vol. 1, *Thinking*. San Diego: Harcourt Brace Jovanovich, 1978.

Aristotle. *Ethics*. Charleston: BiblioBazaar, 2007.

Augustine. *The City of God*. Translated and edited by Marcus Dods. New York: Hafner, 1948.

———. *Confessions*. Translated by R. S. Pine-Coffin. London: Penguin, 1961.

———. "De praedestinatione sanctorum [On the Predestination of Saints]." In *Basic Writings of Saint Augustine*, translated and edited by R. E. Wallis in W. Oates, Vol. 1, 775–817. New York: Random House, 1948.

———. *De Trinitate* [*The Trinity*]. Turnhout, Belgium: Brepolis, 1968.

Bailey, Ronald, and Nick Gillespie. "Biology vs. the Blank Slate: Evolutionary Psychologist Stephen Pinker Deconstructs the Great Myths about How the Mind Works." *Reason*, October 2002. Online: http://www.reason.com/news/show/28537.html.

Benedict XVI. "Faith, Reason and the University: Memories and Reflections." Papal address, "Three Stages in the Program of De-Hellenization," University of Regensburg, Germany, September 12, 2006. Online: http://www.zenit.org/article -16955?l=english.

——— (Joseph Ratzinger). *Milestones: Memoirs, 1927–1977*. Translated by Erasmo Leiva-Merikakis. San Francisco: Ignatius, 1998.

Bercovitch, Sacvan. *The American Jeremiad*. Madison, WI: University of Wisconsin Press, 1978.

Berger, Peter L., editor. *The Desecularization of the World: Resurgent Religion and World Politics*. Grand Rapids: Eerdmans, 1999.

Berry, Wendell. *Given Poems*. Berkeley, CA: Shoemaker & Hoard, 2005.

———. *The Unsettling of America: Culture & Agriculture*. San Francisco: Sierra Club Books, 1977.

Blondel, Maurice. "The Letter on Apologetics." In *The Letter on Apologetics, and, History and Dogma*, translated by Alexander Dru and Illtyd Trethowan, 125–210. Grand Rapids: Eerdmans, 1994.

Boethius. *The Consolation of Philosophy*. Translated by Wilbraham Villiers. London: J. M. Dent, 1902.

Bonhoeffer, Dietrich. *Ethics*. New York: Touchstone, [1949] 1995.

Bradley, Ian C. *Colonies of Heaven: Celtic Christian Communities: Live the Tradition*. Kelowna, BC: Northstone, 2000.

Bremmer, Jan. "Atheism in Antiquity." In *The Cambridge Companion to Atheism*, edited by Michael Martin, 11–26. New York: Cambridge University Press, 2007.

Brooks, Rodney Allen. *Flesh and Machines: How Robots Will Change Us*. New York: Pantheon, 2002.

Buckley, Michael J. *At the Origins of Modern Atheism*. New Haven, CT: Yale University Press, 1987.

Bulgakov, Michael. *The Master and Margarita*. New York: Vintage, 1938.

Calvin, John. *Institutes of the Christian Religion*. 2 vols. 6th American ed. Philadelphia: Presbyterian Board of Publication and Sabbath-School Work, 1921.

Caputo, John D. *More Radical Hermeneutics: On Not Knowing Who We Are*. Bloomington: Indiana University Press, 2000.

———. *Philosophy and Theology*. Nashville: Abingdon, 2006.

Casanova, José. *Public Religions in the Modern World*. Chicago: University of Chicago Press, 1994.

Cavanaugh, William. "Killing for the Telephone Company: Why the Nation State Is Not the Keeper of the Common Good." *Modern Theology* 20 (2004) 243–74.

Cavell, Stanley. *Must We Mean What We Say?: A Book of Essays*. Cambridge: Cambridge University Press, 2002.

Claudel, Paul. *Le soulier de satin ou le pire n'est pas toujours sur*. Paris: Gallimard, 1997.

Cleese, John. "The Scientist at Work." Podcast 32. Online: http://www.johncleesepodcast .co.uk/cleeseblog/.

Collingwood, R. G. *An Essay on Metaphysics*. Oxford: Clarendon, 1940.

Connolly, William E. *Why I Am Not a Secularist*. Minneapolis: University of Minnesota Press, 1999.

Dawkins, Richard. *A Devil's Chaplain: Reflections on Hope, Lies, Science and Love*. New York: Houghton Mifflin, 2003.

———. *The God Delusion*. New York: Houghton Mifflin, 2006.

De Graaf, John, et al. *Affluenza: The All Consuming Epidemic*. San Francisco: Berrett-Koehler, 2001.

Dennett, Daniel Clement. *Breaking the Spell: Religion as a Natural Phenomenon*. New York: Viking, 2006.

————, and Asbjørn Steglich-Petersen, editors. *The Philosophical Lexicon*. 2008. Online: http://www.philosophicallexicon.com/.

Derrida, Jacques. *Acts of Religion*. Translated and edited by Gil Anidjar. New York: Routledge, 2002.

————. *Archive Fever: A Freudian Impression*. Translated by Eric Prenowitz. Chicago: University of Chicago Press, 1996.

————. "Circumfession." In *Jacques Derrida*, by Geoffrey Bennington and Jacques Derrida, translated by Geoffrey Bennington, 3–315. Chicago: University of Chicago Press, 1993.

————. *The Gift of Death*. Translated by David Wills. Chicago: University of Chicago Press, 1996.

————. *Given Time: I: Counterfeit Money*. Translated by Peggy Kamuf. Chicago: University of Chicago Press, 1991.

————. "Khora." In *On the Name*, edited by Thomas Dutoit, translated by David Wood et al., 89–130. Meridian: Crossing Aesthetics. Stanford: Stanford University Press, 1995.

————. *Margins of Philosophy*. Translated by Alan Bass. Chicago: University of Chicago Press, 1982.

————. *Of Grammatology*. Translated by Gayatri Chakravorty Spivak. Baltimore: Johns Hopkins University Press, 1997.

————. *On the Name*. Edited by Thomas Dutoit, translated by David Wood et al. Stanford: Stanford University Press, 1995.

————. *Speech and Phenomena, and Other Essays on Husserl's Theory of Signs*. Translated by David B. Allision. Evanston, IL: Northwestern University Press, 1973.

————. "To Forgive: The Unforgivable and the Imprescriptible." In *Questioning God*, edited by John D. Caputo, Mark Dooley, and Michael J. Scanlon, 21–51. Bloomington: Indiana University Press, 2001.

————. "Villanova, Prés de Philadelphia, le 26 Septembre, 1997." In *La Contra-Allée*, by Jacques Derrida and Catherine Malabou, 99–102. Paris: La Quinzaine Littéraire, 1999.

————. *Writing and Difference*. Translated by Alan Bass. Chicago: University of Chicago Press, 1978.

Desmond, William. *Being and the Between*. Albany: SUNY Press, 1995.

Dews, Peter. *Logics of Disintegration: Post-Structuralist Thought and the Claims of Critical Theory*. London: Verso, 1987.

Duffy, Eamon. *Saints and Sinners: A History of the Popes*. New Haven, CT: Yale University Press, 1997.

Dylan, Bob. "It's Alright, Ma (I'm Only Bleeding)." *Bringing It All Back Home*. Columbia, 1965.

Eagleton, Terry. *Reason, Faith, and Revolution: Reflections on the God Debate*. New Haven, CT: Yale University Press, 2009.

Edgell, Penny, et al. "Atheists as 'Other': Moral Boundaries and Cultural Membership in American Society." *American Sociological Review* 71 (2006) 211–34.

Fee, Gordon D., and Mark L. Strauss. *How to Choose a Translation for All Its Worth: A Guide to Understanding and Using Bible Versions.* Grand Rapids: Zondervan, 2007.

Fish, Stanley. "God Talk." *New York Times,* Think Again blog, May 3, 2009. Online: http://fish.blogs.nytimes.com/2009/05/03/god-talk/.

———. "God Talk, Part 2." *New York Times,* Think Again blog, May 17, 2009. Online: http://fish.blogs.nytimes.com/2009/05/17/god-talk-part-2/.

———. *How Milton Works.* Cambridge, MA: Harvard University Press, 2003.

Flew, Antony. *There Is a God: How the World's Most Notorious Atheist Changed His Mind.* New York: HarperOne, 2007.

———, and Gary Habermas. "My Pilgrimage from Atheism to Theism. A Discussion between Antony Flew and Gary Habermas." *Philosophia Christi* 6:2 (2004) 197–211.

Gilbert, William, and Arthur Sullivan. *The Pirates of Penzance.* Whitefish, MT: Kessinger, [1879] 2005.

Girard, René. "The Founding Murder in the Philosophy of Nietzsche." In *Violence and Truth: On the Work of René Girard,* edited by Paul Dumouchel, 227–46. London: Athlone, 1988.

Giussani, Luigi. *The Risk of Education.* Translated by Rosanna M. Giammanco Frongia. New York: Crossroad, 2001.

Goudzwaard, Bob, Mark Vander Vennen, and David Van Heemst. *Hope in Troubled Times: A New Vision for Confronting Global Crises.* Grand Rapids: Baker Academic, 2007.

Guinness, Os. *The Gravedigger File: Papers on the Subversion of the Modern Church.* London: Hodder and Stoughton, 1983.

Habermas, Jürgen. "Faith and Knowledge." In *The Frankfurt School on Religion: Key Writings by the Major Thinkers,* edited by Eduardo Mendieta, 327–38. New York: Routledge, 2005.

———. "Israel or Athens: Where Does Anamnestic Reason Belong?" In *The Liberating Power of Symbols: Philosophical Essays,* translated by Peter Dews, 1–29. Cambridge: MIT Press, 2001.

Harris, Sam. *End of Faith: Religion, Terror, and the Future of Reason.* New York: Norton, 2004.

———. *Letter to a Christian Nation.* New York: Knopf, 2006.

Hart, David Bentley. *Atheist Delusions: The Christian Revolution and Its Fashionable Enemies.* New Haven, CT: Yale University Press, 2009.

———. *The Beauty of the Infinite: The Aesthetics of Christian Truth.* Grand Rapids: Eerdmans, 2003.

Hart, Hendrik. "The Spirit of God and the Times of Our Lives." Exaugural address, Institute for Christian Studies convocation, November 30, 2001.

Helmick, Raymond G., and Rodney L. Petersen, editors. *Forgiveness and Reconciliation: Religion, Public Policy & Conflict Transformation.* Philadelphia: Templeton Foundation Press, 2001.

Hertzke, Allen D. *Representing God in Washington: The Role of Religious Lobbies in American Polity.* Knoxville: University of Tennessee Press, 1988.

Hervieu-Léger, Danièle. *Religion as a Chain of Memory*. Translated by Simon Lee. Cambridge, UK: Polity, 2000.

Hitchens, Christopher. *God Is Not Great: How Religion Poisons Everything*. New York: Twelve, 2007.

Hopkins, Gerard Manley. "God's Grandeur." In *The Major Works*, edited by Catherine Philliops, 128. Oxford: Oxford University Press, 2002.

Horkheimer, Max, and Theodor W. Adorno. *Dialectic of Enlightenment: Philosophical Fragments*. Edited by Gunzelin Schmid Noerr, translated by Edmund Jephcott. Stanford: Stanford University Press, 2002.

Jacoby, Susan. *Freethinkers: A History of American Secularism*. New York: Holt, 2004.

Jaspers, Karl. *Nietzsche: An Introduction to the Understanding of His Philosophical Activity*. Translated by Charles F. Wallraff and Frederick J. Schmitz. 3rd ed. South Bend, IN: Gateway, 1979.

Kavanaugh, Kieran. Introduction to *The Collected Works of Saint John of the Cross*, translated by Kieran Kavanaugh and Otilio Rodriguez, 1–22. Rev. ed. Washington, DC: Institute of Carmelite Studies Publications, 1991.

Kierkegaard, Søren. *Attack upon Christendom*. Translated by Walter Lawrie. Princeton: Princeton University Press, 1948.

———. *Fear and Trembling*. Translated by Howard V. Hong and Edna H. Hong. Princeton: Princeton University Press, 1983.

Kristeva, Julia. *Strangers to Ourselves*. Translated by Leon S. Roudiez. London: Harvester, 1991.

Lash, Nicholas. "Among Strangers and Friends: Thinking of God in Our Current Confusion." In *Finding God in All Things: Essays in Honor of Michael J. Buckley*, edited by Michael J. Himes and Stephen J. Pope, 53–67. New York: Crossroad, 1996.

Lewis, C. S. "Learning in War-time." In *The Weight of Glory and Other Addresses*, 43–54. Grand Rapids: Eerdmans, 1979.

———. *Miracles: A Preliminary Study*. New York: HarperCollins, [1947], 2001.

———. *The Problem of Pain*. New York: HarperCollins, [1940], 1996.

Lubac, Henri de. *The Drama of Atheist Humanism*. San Francisco: Ignatius, 1995.

Luther, Martin. *Luther's Works*. Vol. 12: *Selected Psalms I*. Edited by Jaroslav Pelikan. St. Louis: Concordia, 1955.

Manent, Pierre. *An Intellectual History of Liberalism*. Translated by Rebecca Balinski. Princeton: Princeton University Press, 1995.

Marsden, George. *Fundamentalism and American Culture*. 2nd ed. New York: Oxford University Press, 2006.

The Martyrdom of St. Polycarp. In *The Didache, The Epistle of Barnabas, The Epistles and The Martyrdom of St. Polycarp, The Fragments of Papias, The Epistle to Diognetus*, translated by James A. Kleist, 90–102. Ancient Christian Writers 6. Westminster, MD: Newman, 1948.

Marx, Karl, and Friedrich Engels. *Manifesto of the Communist Party* (1848). Marxists Internet Archive, 2000. Online: http://www.marxists.org/archive/marx/works/1848/communist-manifesto/index.htm.

Mathewes, Charles, and Christopher McKnight Nichols, editors. *Prophesies of Godlessness: Predictions of America's Imminent Secularization, from the Puritans to the Present Day*. New York: Oxford University Press, 2008.

Mavrodes, George. *Belief in God: A Study in the Epistemology of Religion*. New York: Random House, 1970.

———. "On the Very Strongest Arguments." In *Prospects for Natural Theology*, edited by Eugene Thomas Long, 81–91. Studies in Philosophy and the History of Philosophy 25. Washington, DC: Catholic University of America Press, 1992.

McCarraher, Eugene. "The Enchantments of Mammon." *Modern Theology* 21 (July 2005) 429–61.

McKibben, Bill. *Enough: Staying Human in an Engineered Age*. New York: Times Books, 2003.

McLaren, Brian D. *Everything Must Change: Jesus, Global Crises, and a Revolution of Hope*. Nashville: Thomas Nelson, 2007.

Merton, Thomas. "Apologies to an Unbeliever." In *Faith and Violence: Christian Teaching and Christian Practice*, 205–14. Notre Dame: University of Notre Dame Press, 1968.

———. *Contemplation in a World of Action*. Notre Dame: University of Notre Dame Press, 1998.

Milbank, John. *Theology and Social Theory: Beyond Secular Reason*. 2nd ed. Oxford: Blackwell, 2006.

Miller, Trevor. "Introduction." Rule of the Northumbria Community. Online: http://northumbriacommunity.org/WhoWeAre/whoweareTheRule2.htm.

Milton, John. *Areopagitica: A Speech of Mr. John Milton for the Liberty of Unlicensed Printing to the Parliament of England*. Clark, NJ: Lawbook Exchange, 2006.

———. *Paradise Lost*. Edited by John Leonard. New York: Penguin Classics, 2003.

Moltmann, Jürgen. "Introduction." In *Man on His Own: Essays in the Philosophy of Religion*, by Ernst Bloch, translated by E. B. Ashton, 19–29. New York: Herder, 1970.

Muralt, André de. *L'unité de la philosophie politique: De Scot, Occam et Suarez, au libéralisme contemporain*. Paris: Vrin, 2002.

Nielsen, Kai, and Hendrik Hart. *Search for Community in a Withering Tradition: Conversations between a Marxian Atheist and a Calvinian Christian*. Lanham, MD: University Press of America, 1990.

Nietzsche, Friedrich. *Beyond Good and Evil: Prelude to a Philosophy of the Future*. Translated by Walter Kaufman. New York: Vintage, 1966.

———. *The Gay Science*. Translated by Walter Kaufmann. New York: Vintage, 1974.

———. *On the Genealogy of Morality*. Edited by Kieth Ansell-Pearson, translated by Carol Diethe. Cambridge: Cambridge University Press, 1994.

———. *Will to Power*. Edited by Walter Kauffman, translated by Walter Kauffman and R. J. Hollingdale. New York: Vintage, 1967.

Noll, Mark. *The Scandal of the Evangelical Mind*. Grand Rapids: Eerdmans, 1994.

O'Connor, Flannery. *The Habit of Being*. Edited by Sally Fitzgerald. New York: Farrar, Straus, Giroux, 1978.

Olthuis, James H. "Be(com)ing Humankind as Gift and Call." *Philosophia Reformata* 58 (1993) 153–72.

Onfray, Michel. *Atheist Manifesto: The Case against Christianity, Judaism, and Islam.* Translated by Jeremy Leggatt. New York: Arcade, 2007.

Percy, Walker. "Why Are You a Catholic?" In *Signposts in a Strange Land*, edited by Patrick Samway, 304–15. New York: Farrar, Straus, and Giroux, 1991.

Peterson, Eugene H. *A Long Obedience in the Same Direction: Discipleship in an Instant Society*. Downers Grove, IL: InterVarsity, 1980.

Pieper, Josef. *Leisure, the Basis of Culture*. Translated by Gerald Malsbary. South Bend, IN: St. Augustine's, 1998.

Plantinga, Alvin. *God, Freedom, and Evil*. Grand Rapids: Eerdmans, 1977.

———. "Reason and Belief in God." In *Faith and Rationality: Reason and Belief in God*, edited by Alvin Plantinga and Nicholas Wolterstorff, 74–78. Notre Dame: Notre Dame University Press, 1983.

Polyani, Karl. *The Great Transformation*. Boston: Beacon, [1944] 2001.

Pullman, Philip. *The Amber Spyglass*. New York: Knopf, 2000.

———. *The Subtle Knife*. New York: Knopf, 1997.

Raboteau, Albert J. *Slave Religion: The "Invisible Institution" in the Antebellum South*. New York: Oxford University Press, 1978.

Rawls, John. *Political Liberalism*. New York: Columbia University Press, 1993.

Retort (Iain Boal, T. J. Clark, Joseph Matthews, and Michael Watts). *Afflicted Powers: Capital and Spectacle in a New Age of War*. London: Verso, 2005.

Ricoeur, Paul. *Freud and Philosophy: An Essay on Interpretation*. Translated by Denis Savage. New Haven, CT: Yale University Press, 1970.

———. "Hermeneutics and the Critique of Ideology." In *From Text to Action*, translated by Kathleen Blamey and John B. Thompson, 270–307. Essays in Hermeneutics 2. Evanston, IL: Northwestern University Press, 1991.

———. *Time and Narrative*. Vol. 3. Translated by Kathleen Blamey and David Pellauer. Chicago: University of Chicago Press, 1988.

Rilke, Rainer Maria. "The First Elegy." In *Duino Elegies and The Sonnets to Orpheus*, translated by A. Poulin Jr., 5–12. New York: First Mariner, 2005.

Robinson, John A. T. "The End of Theism?" In *Honest to God*, 29–44. London: SCM, 1963.

Runner, H. Evan. *The Relation of the Bible to Learning*. Toronto: Wedge, 1970.

Shakespeare, William. *Hamlet*. Edited by Ann Thompson and Neil Taylor. Arden Shakespeare, 3rd ser. London: Cengage Learning, 2006.

———. *Macbeth*. Edited by Alfred Harbage. Baltimore: Penguin, 1971.

Sheehan, Jonathan. "Framing the Middle." Review of *A Secular Age* by Charles Taylor. The Immanent Frame, January 14, 2008. Online: http://www.ssrc.org/blogs/immanent _frame/2008/01/14/framing-the-middle/.

Sittser, Gerald L. *Water from a Deep Well*. Downers Grove, IL: InterVarsity, 2007.

Smith, Christian, editor. *The Secular Revolution: Power, Interests, and Conflict in the Secularization of American Public Life*. Berkeley: University of California Press, 2003.

Smith, James K. A. "Determined Violence: Derrida's Structural Religion," *Journal of Religion* 78 (1998) 197–212.

———. "Re-Kanting Postmodernism?: Derrida's Religion within the Limits of Reason Alone." *Faith and Philosophy* 17 (2000) 558–71.

Smith, Quentin. "The Metaphilosophy of Naturalism," *Philo* 4:2 (2001) 7–20.

Stout, Jeffrey. *Democracy and Tradition*. Princeton: Princeton University Press, 2004.

Taylor, Charles. *A Secular Age*. Cambridge: Belknap Press of Harvard University Press, 2007.

———. "Secularism and Critique." The Immanent Frame, April 24, 2008. Online: http://www.ssrc.org/blogs/immanent_frame/2008/04/24/secularism-and-critique/.

Thompson, Leonard L. "The Martyrdom of Polycarp: Death in the Roman Games." *The Journal of Religion* 82 (2002) 27–52.

Tilly, Charles. "War Making and State Making as Organized Crime." In *Bringing the State Back In*, edited by Peter B. Evans, Dietrich Rueschemeyer, and Theda Skocpol, 169–91. New York: Cambridge University Press, 1985.

Tomlinson, Dave. *The Post Evangelical*. Rev. North American ed. El Cajon, CA: Emergent YS, 2003.

Toulmin, Stephen Edelston. *Cosmopolis: The Hidden Agenda of Modernity*. Chicago: University of Chicago Press, 1990.

Twells, Henry. "Not for Our Sins Alone" (1889). In *Rejoice in the Lord: A Hymn Companion to the Scriptures*, edited by Erik Routley, no. 506, 5. Grand Rapids: Eerdmans, 1985.

Updike, John. *In the Beauty of the Lilies*. New York: Knopf, 1996.

Vander Goot, Henry, editor. *Life Is Religion: Essays in Honor of H. Evan Runner*. St. Catharines, ON: Paideia, 1981.

Walsh, Brian J., and J. Richard Middleton. *The Transforming Vision: Shaping a Christian World View*. Downers Grove, IL: InterVarsity, 1984.

Webber, Robert E. *The Younger Evangelicals: Facing the Challenges of the New World*. Grand Rapids: Baker, 2002.

Weber, Max. "Science as Vocation." In *From Max Weber: Essays in Sociology*, edited and translated by H. H. Gerth and C. Wright Mills, 129–58. Oxford: Oxford University Press, 1946.

Westphal, Merold. *Suspicion and Faith: The Religious Uses of Modern Atheism*. Bronx, NY: Fordham University Press, 1998.

Wirzba, Norman. *The Paradise of God: Renewing Religion in an Ecological Age*. Oxford: Oxford University Press, 2003.

Wittgenstein, Ludwig. *Remarks on Fraser's Golden Bough*. Edited by Rush Rhees. Nottinghamshire, UK: Brynmill, 1971.

Wright, N. T. "God." In *Simply Christian: Why Christianity Makes Sense*, 55–70. San Francisco: HarperSanFrancisco, 2006.

———. *The New Testament and the People of God*. Christian Origins and the Question of God 1. Minneapolis: Fortress, 1992.

———. *Surprised by Hope: Rethinking Heaven, the Resurrection, and the Mission of the Church*. New York: HarperOne, 2008.

Wykstra, Stephen. "Toward a Sensible Evidentialism: On the Notion of 'Needing Evidence.'" In *Philosophy of Religion: Selected Readings*, edited by William L. Rowe and William J. Wainwright, 426–37. 2nd ed. San Diego: Harcourt Brace Jovanovich, 1989.

Žižek, Slavoj. "Defenders of the Faith." *New York Times*, Op-ed, March 12, 2006.

———. *The Fragile Absolute, or, Why Is the Christian Legacy Worth Fighting For?* London: Verso, 2000.

———. *The Puppet and the Dwarf: The Perverse Core of Christianity*. Cambridge: The MIT Press, 2003.

Contributors

Andy Barnes lives with his wife outside of Washington, DC. He holds a master of arts in literature from Rutgers University and is a former reviews editor for *The Other Journal*.

Peter M. Candler Jr. is associate professor of theology in the Honors College at Baylor University. He is the author of *Theology, Rhetoric, Manuduction, or, Reading Scripture Together on the Path to God* (2006) and *Thomism: A Very Critical Introduction* (forthcoming). A native of Atlanta, Georgia, he lives in Texas with his wife, Meredith, their sons, Henry and Charles, and two maladjusted quadrupeds.

Becky Crook has written poetry, reviews, and interviews for *The Other Journal* where she previously served as a creative writing editor. With a background in linguistics, European studies, and Christian Scriptures, she is an occasional poet and frequent bicycle rider whose most recent practice of abandon includes moving to Berlin, Germany, in pursuit of love, language, and new forests to explore.

Brad Davis is author of a four-book, 150-poem sequence that converses with the Psalms. His poems have appeared in *Poetry*, *The Paris Review*, *Tar River Poetry*, *Image*, *Connecticut Review*, and elsewhere, and he has received the AWP Intro Journal Award, the Sunken Garden Poetry Prize, and the International Arts Movement's Poetry Award. Davis divides his time between directing the Manor Institute on Shelter Island, New York, editing the *Broken Bridge Review* in Pomfret, Connecticut, and visiting family in Brooklyn, New York.

Courtney Druz is a Jewish poet and mother of three in New Jersey. She has previously worked as an architect and graphic designer, and she holds a master of architecture from the University of Pennsylvania. Her poems have appeared in a variety of print and online publications, including *Drash, New Vilna Review, Prick of the Spindle*, and *Zeek*.

Stanley Fish is the Davidson-Kahn Distinguished University Professor and a professor of law at Florida International University. He has previously taught at the University of California at Berkeley, John Hopkins University, Duke University, and the University of Illinois at Chicago, where he was dean of the College of Liberal Arts and Sciences. He has received many honors and awards, including being named the Chicagoan of the Year for Culture. Fish is the author of ten books and is now a weekly columnist for the *New York Times*. He resides in Andes, New York, and Delray Beach, Florida, with his wife, Jane Tompkins.

Brandi Gentry's poetry has appeared in *Conceptions Southwest* and *The Other Journal*. She is working toward a master of fine arts in poetry at Warren Wilson College. Gentry currently lives in Oklahoma with her husband and two daughters.

Larry Gilman lives with his wife in the hills of Vermont. He was trained as an electrical engineer but has since opted for a life of freelance writing and editing. He is Episcopalian.

Stanley Hauerwas is the Gilbert T. Rowe Professor of Theological Ethics at the Divinity School of Duke University. Though Hauerwas is often identified as an ethicist, his work is more properly described as theology—his primary intent being to show how theological convictions make no sense unless they are actually embodied in our lives. His work draws on a great range of literature, from classical, philosophical, and theological texts to contemporary political theory. His most recent publications include *The State of the University: Academic Knowledges and the Knowledge of God* (2007) and *A Cross-Shattered Church: Reclaiming the Theological Heart of Preaching* (2009).

Robert Inchausti is professor of English at California State Polytechnic University at San Luis Obispo. He is the author of *Subversive Orthodoxy: Outlaws, Revolutionaries, and Other Christians in Disguise* (2005), *The Ignorant Perfection of Ordinary People* (1991), *Spitwad Sutras: Classroom*

Teaching as Sublime Vocation (1993), and *Thomas Merton's American Prophecy* (1998).

Ronald A. Kuipers is assistant professor of philosophy of religion at the Institute for Christian Studies. He is the author of *Critical Faith: Toward a Renewed Understanding of Religious Life and Its Public Accountability* (2002) and *Solidarity and the Stranger: Themes in the Social Philosophy of Richard Rorty* (1997). His current research explores the increasing dialogical traffic between secular and religious philosophers in the early twenty-first century. Away from the wild world of philosophy, he can usually be found at the hockey rink, renovating his house, or spending idle time with his wife, Cheryl, and two kids, Olivia and Ben.

D. Stephen Long is professor of systematic theology at Marquette University. His most recent publication is *Speaking of God: Theology, Language, and Truth* (2009).

Charles T. Mathewes is associate professor of religious ethics and history of Christian thought at the University of Virginia. He is editor of the *Journal of the American Academy of Religion*, the author of *Evil and the Augustinian Tradition* (2001) and *A Theology of Public Life* (2007), and with Chris Nichols was the co-editor of *Prophesies of Godlessness: Predictions of America's Imminent Secularization, from the Puritans to the Present Day* (2008). His forthcoming book is entitled *The Republic of Grace: Augustinian Thoughts for Dark Times.*

John Milbank is research professor of religion, politics, and ethics and director of the Centre of Theology and Philosophy at the University of Nottingham, having previously taught at Lancaster, Cambridge, and the University of Virginia. Milbank is the co-founder of Radical Orthodoxy and the author of many works including *Theology and Social Theory: Beyond Secular Reason* (1991), *The Legend of Death: Two Poetic Sequences* (2008), *The Future of Love: Essays in Political Theology* (2009), and most recently, *The Monstrosity of Christ: Paradox or Dialectic?* (2009) with Slavoj Žižek. Along with Catherine Pickstock and Graham Ward, he is editor of the *Illuminations* series for Blackwell.

Randal Rauser is associate professor of historical theology at Taylor Seminary. He is author of *Theology in Search of Foundations* (2009), *Finding God in the Shack* (2009), and *Faith Lacking Understanding: Theology "Through a Glass, Darkly"'* (2008). He is married to Jasper, has one daughter, Jamie, and a Lhasa apso named Sonny.

Dan Rhodes is a pastor at Emmaus Way, a doctoral student in theology at Duke Divinity School, and a theology editor for *The Other Journal*. He lives in Durham, North Carolina.

Paul Roorda lives in Kitchener, Ontario, and has had exhibitions at the Toronto School of Theology, the Institute for Christian Studies, and Wilfrid Laurier University. He was the artist in residence for the city of Kitchener in 2007 and has been the subject of an episode of *The Artist's Life*, which aired on Bravo TV. Roorda's work is found in numerous collections, including the University of Waterloo and the Donovan Collection at the University of Toronto.

Christine Sine is an Australian physician and author of *Godspace: Finding Peace in the Rhythms of Life* (2006). She lives in Seattle, Washington, with her husband, Tom, and dog, Bonnie, and she works as executive director for Mustard Seed Associates. She is a passionate organic gardener, knitter, and blogger.

Luci Shaw is the author of ten volumes of poetry, including *What the Light Was Like* (2006), *Accompanied by Angels: Poems of the Incarnation* (2006), and *The Genesis of It All* (2006), and the nonfiction prose books *The Crime of Living Cautiously: Hearing God's Call to Adventure* (2005) and *Breath for the Bones: Art, Imagination, and Spirit* (2007). She is writer in residence at Regent College, and her poetry has appeared in *Weavings, Image, Books & Culture, The Christian Century, Rock & Sling, Radix, Ruminate, Crux, Stonework, Nimble Spirit, The Southern Review*, and others.

Jon Stanley is currently completing his doctorate of philosophy in philosophical theology at the Institute for Christian Studies. His work interfaces with philosophy, theology, and anthropology and draws Reformational theology into dialogue with other theological traditions and contemporary movements. His current project explores the metaphorics of both Radical Orthodoxy and the Reformational tradition in order to reimagine the meaning of religion in terms of "covenantal participation." Stanley is also a practicing psychotherapist and serves as theology editor for *The Other Journal*. He lives in Toronto with his partner, Julie, and daughter, Caedance.

Ben Suriano is a theology editor for *The Other Journal*. He is currently working on his doctorate of philosophy at Marquette University, where he is studying the relationship between metaphysics and politics in both the theology and philosophy departments. He is especially interested in exploring the relationship between the production of the bourgeois subject and the rise to prominence of Western atheism, as well as how a theological materialism might make sense.

Charles Taylor is professor emeritus of philosophy at McGill University and winner of the 2007 Templeton Prize. He is author of many books, including *Sources of the Self: The Making of Modern Identity* (1989) and *A Secular Age* (2007).

Merold Westphal is distinguished professor of philosophy at Fordham University. He is the author of numerous articles and books, many of them in continental philosophy of religion. His newest books are *Levinas and Kierkegaard in Dialogue* (2008) and *Whose Community? Which Interpretation? Philosophical Hermeneutics for the Church* (2009).